TECHNOLOGY TRANSFORMING 2013 AND BEYOND

SWANEPOEL

TECHNOLOGY REPORT 2013

Stefan J. M. Swanepoel
with
co-author Michael McClure
and contributors
Sean Carpenter, Jeff Lobb, Kelly Mitchell,
Chris Nichols, Jay Thompson, Krisstina Wise and Kendyl Young

SWANEPOEL TECHNOLOGY REPORT

MANGING AUTHOR
Stefan J.M. Swanepoel

CO-AUTHOR
Michael McClure

CONTRIBUTORS
S. Carpenter, J. Lobb,
K. Mitchell, C. Nichols,
J. Thompson, K. Wise
and K. Young

EDITOR
Thomas M. Mitchell

GRAPHICS
Christopher Long

COVER
D.J. Swanepoel

LAYOUT AND DESIGN
Tinus Swanepoel

ISBN
978-0-970-4523-6-8

PRICING
$ 149.95 USA $ 149.95 CAN   € 114.95 EUR

BOOKS AND REPORTS BY THE AUTHOR

- *Real Estate Handbook (1987)*
- *A New Era in Real Estate (1990)*
- *Swanepoel Top Real Estate Firms (1993)*
- *Real Estate Confronts Reality (1997)*
- *Real Estate Confronts Technology (1999)*
- *Real Estate Confronts the e-Consumer (2000)*
- *Real Estate Confronts the Banks (2001)*
- *Real Estate Confronts Profitability (2003)*
- *Real Estate Confronts Customer Acquisition (2004)*
- *Real Estate Confronts the Future (2004)*
- *The Domino Effect (2005)*
- *Real Estate Confronts Bundled Services (2005)*
- *Real Estate Confronts Goal Setting vs. Business Planning (2006)*
- *Swanepoel TRENDS Report (2006 Edition)*
- *Real Estate Confronts the Information Explosion (2007)*
- *Swanepoel TRENDS Report (2007 Edition)*
- *Swanepoel TRENDS Report (2008 Edition)*
- *Swanepoel TRENDS Report (2009 Edition)*
- *Swanepoel SOCIAL MEDIA Report (2010 Edition)*
- *Swanepoel TRENDS Report (2010 Edition)*
- *Swanepoel TRENDS Report (2011 Edition)*
- *Surviving Your Serengeti: 7 Skills to Master Business & Life (2011)*
- *Swanepoel TRENDS Report (2012 Edition)*
- *Swanepoel TRENDS Report (2013 Edition)*
- *Swanepoel TECHNOLOGY Report (2013 Edition)*

OWNER AND PUBLISHER
RealSure, Inc.
P O Box 7259
Laguna Niguel, CA 92607
Tel: 949.681.9409
www.RETrends.com

Table of Contents

Blogging: The Key to Prospecting, Networking and Building Relationships. Blogging may very well be real estate's largest lead generation play. With so many people starting their search for homes online you need a method and a place to connect with those people, and to expand your client base and your future income pipeline. A blog can be a great tool to capture and nurture leads..

Podcasting: An Opportunity of Episodic Nature. The Web is a crowded place. So the best place to have the largest impact is where you can stand out. And the one place where not many real estate agents have yet ventured is podcasting. With its low barrier to entry this can be a great way for you to demonstrate real expertise and create amazing top-of-mind awareness in your market.

Twitter: The World's Greatest Relationship Creation Machine. There is more often than not a strong correlation between the size of your network and the size of your income. Twitter can open the door quickly to a huge pool of 500 million users. Learn how to leverage this rapidly expanding and unique platform to grow your network faster than most other ways.

Video: The Next Big Thing in Real Estate. YouTube is now the #2 search engine behind only Google, and video is the new normal for almost everything. Both buyers and sellers have endless reasons they like video. Video usage in real estate is expected to grow exponentially in the coming decade as video technology keeps getting cheaper and easier to use.

Online Reputation: The Importance of Integrity and Transparency. From hotels to restaurants to movies, and from Yelp to Amazon to Angie's List, "Googling someone" has become the norm. Ratings and reviews are rapidly becoming ubiquitous. What do people find when they Google YOU? Here is what you should do to ensure you make the best impression online.

Table of Contents

Table of Contents

Foreword

Nearly every single industry and business model will be upended by the Smartphone. We've lived through two previous consumer technology revolutions whose magnitude has been similarly seismic: the ascendancy of the personal computer beginning in the early 80s, and the mainstreaming of the World Wide Web in the late 90s. Each of those revolutions had massive impacts, but this one will be bigger.

According to Strategy Analytics, global Smartphone shipments grew annually by 43 percent to a record 700 million units in 2012. A report by Cisco states global mobile data traffic in 2012 was nearly twelve times the size of the entire global Internet in 2000, with average Smartphone usage growing 81 percent in 2012. Smartphones are everywhere, and we're using them for everything.

Already technology companies that we would have described as "dot-coms" in years past are getting more than half of their usage from mobile devices; more than 680 million users access Facebook on a mobile device each month. Web services from Facebook to Twitter to eBay have all seen their mobile usage skyrocket. In the real estate space, Zillow's mobile usage in January 2012 was larger than all Zillow usage (mobile + desktop) just two years earlier in January 2010.

To get a sense for how the Smartphone revolution is changing an industry, let's look at the restaurant industry. Like real estate, the restaurant industry is very competitive, highly fragmented and made up of hundreds of thousands of entrepreneurial small business owners.

In just the past few years the Smartphone has affected many parts of this centuries-old industry. It changed the way diners make reservations: OpenTable connected more than 100 million diners with restaurants last year, and about 30 percent of their reservations are now made via Smartphone.

The Smartphone is also changing the take-out part of the restaurant industry, with GrubHub and Seamless both driving huge take-out volumes to restaurants on their mobile apps. And the software tools made available to restaurant owners are changing business operations as well, allowing them to track their results in real-time, manage their supply chain and even schedule their staff—all from a Smartphone.

Now let's look at real estate. The personal computer revolution allowed us to create giant repositories of listings data (MLS). Two decades later the Internet revolution empowered consumers by allowing them to access listings data themselves, which changed the role of the real estate agent from information gatekeeper to trusted advisor. The current mobile revolution takes this trend even further, since the home shopper is now armed with home photos, listings information, price history, home valuation data, school reviews, neighborhood data and much more. The successful agent, not to be outdone in this arms race, is equally well equipped with mobile housing data and productivity software to make her more helpful and efficient.

The rate of growth of technology is dizzying, and makes it incredibly challenging for those of us with day jobs to keep up. Further complicating the situation, we may all be working for Hal, the famous computer from the film "2001." Marc Andreesen, the creator of Netscape (the first Web browser)

Foreword Continued...

and the über venture capitalist, recently said that the proliferation of computing power, Smartphones and the Web are creating an economy where jobs will fall into two categories: ones in which you tell a computer what to do, and ones in which the computer tells you what to do. That's a scary and somewhat apocalyptical, but incredibly insightful and prescient, vision.

So how can you protect yourself from the insanity?

The solution to all of your technological trepidations is in your hand: this Report. That's right; the world's oldest form of media can help us understand the revolution amongst us. It serves varied needs: from helping you understand what your kids are talking about at the dinner table (if you can even get them to look up from their Smartphone long enough to talk), to helping you grow your business and your career in the face of rapid technological change.

You've already taken the first step toward using the technology revolution to help you grow your business. By reading this Report, you've recognized that technology is something to be practiced, not feared. The only way to ensure that you're in a job where you tell the computer what to do instead of the other way around is to stay ahead of the technological tidal wave.

See you around the Web,

Spencer Rascoff
CEO, Zillow Inc.
@spencerrascoff

Preface

This is a hands-on, practical guide covering the full spectrum of the most important elements of the technologies that directly impact your business: online, social media, mobile and so much more. We've targeted the very things that increasingly shape and transform the real estate industry in which you and I live, work and earn our keep.

Everyone tells us that consumers are changing, that home-buyers and sellers are different and that the real estate transaction will never be the same. And they're right! The industry has become a huge data repository for everything that's real estate and consumers have found it all accessible and useable on their Smartphones and Tablets.

There are a large number of challenges associated with making sense of it: deciding what can be done to maximize the opportunities borne of these significant changes, developing strategies and tactics to capitalize on those opportunities. It's true that we are already able to do every part of the real estate transaction on the road with our iPad or Smartphone—anywhere, anytime—and some of you already are. But there is so much to keep up with, so much to master—so many programs, apps and ways of doing things—all of which are also continuously changing.

Hence the annual *Swanepoel TECHNOLOGY Report*.

This is a companion Report to the annual *Swanepoel TRENDS Report* that is now in its eighth year. Both of these Reports are approximately 164 pages; TRENDS being published at the end January and TECHNOLOGY at the end April. The TRENDS Report focuses on critical industry trends, strategies, management, acquisitions, commissions, business models, office models, etc. The goal of the TECHNOLOGY Report is to research, compile and provide practical guidance to help you decide whether you need any of these new technologies–and, if so, which ones–along with the steps you should follow to implement them. Obviously, one edition will never cover the full range of technologies, so we will every year focus on the 10 most current and significant elements we believe will help you to become a successful online real estate professional.

For example, this year we covered topics such as blogging, podcasting, Twitter, Evernote, video, portals, managing your digital footprint, using Mobile and beginning your journey toward becoming a paperless agent. We researched but, for a variety of reasons, this year elected not to include important technologies such as Facebook, LinkedIn, Instagram, texting, online education and mobile payments. Those subjects will most likely make their way into the 2014 edition of the *Swanepoel TECHNOLOGY Report*. Our vision is to make all Reports dynamic and flexible on thus given the pace at which technologies keep evolving, we're expect we'll be including things in the near future that probably haven't even been invented yet!

In celebration of the fact that the two Reports this year are our 19th and 20th publications tracking real estate trends—that's over 2,000 pages of published trend research on the real estate industry—we've decided to release copies of the last five years of the Swanepoel TRENDS Reports on our website (RETrends.com) as our contribution towards building a better real estate industry. This information is

Preface Continued...

complimentary; it is searchable, viewable in HTML and downloadable in PDF format. Enjoy!

Lastly, to my co-author and contributors, thank you to each and every one of you that shared your knowledge and time to help make this first *Swanepoel TECHNOLOGY Report* as comprehensive as it is. The world of technology is so rapidly evolving and so expansive that I could not have done this without your enormous contribution, knowledge and practical experience. You have my sincere appreciation and gratitude.

On behalf of the co-author and all of the contributors, we hope that your future is wireless, online, connected and integrated!

Stefan Swanepoel
New York Times Best Selling Author
March 2013
@Swanepoel

PS: 2013 will also be the inaugural event of the Swanepoel T3 Summit. This serious — no trade exhibitions, no sales pitches — event is for those visionaries and thought leaders who are interested to debate and network with other like-minded individuals in a non-commercial atmosphere. The T3 Summit is held in April every year. For more details visit T3Summit.com.

Introduction

SWANEPOEL TRENDS REPORT

The RealSure team has been researching and writing about trends impacting the real estate industry since 1997. This is our 20th book/report and we are not aware of any other company that has published more books/reports on this topic.

The original Real Estate Confronts series that started with *Real Estate Confronts Reality* consisted of 10 titles. Since 2006 the *Swanepoel TRENDS Report* has been a constant annual staple for leadership of franchisee groups, broker/owners of real estate brokerage companies, REALTOR® Associations, MLS companies, technology vendors serving the real estate industry, educators and coaches, mortgage companies, title companies and those top producing agents that want to be at the leading edge of change and innovation.

Since its inception various chapters in the *Swanepoel TRENDS Report* have annually dealt with technology, the Internet, e-Commerce, Social Media and mobile technology. Gradually the number of pages dedicated to technology reached a point where it became obvious that there was a need for a separate report covering this vitally important part of the real estate business. Hence the *Swanepoel TECHNOLOGY Report* was born.

CONFIDENTIAL INFORMATION

No confidential sources were used in this Report and no information identified as confidential under any existing NDA was included without permission from the appropriate parties. This Report is a result of extensive research, articles that are readily available through the media, the study of hundreds of websites, Social Media pages, forums, surveys, whitepapers, and one-on-one discussions with industry decision makers, leaders, brokers, agents and vendors.

TRADEMARKS

Most of the companies mentioned in this Report own numerous trademarks and other marks. This Report, the publishers, the author, the contributors or any other party involved in this Report in no way challenges or seeks to dilute any of these marks and acknowledge their ownership. Specifically Realtor® is a registered trademark of the National Association of Realtors®.

FOCUS

Currently the *Swanepoel TRENDS Report* strives to cover issues concerning: strategy, management, business and office models, association leadership, MLS Innovation, mergers and acquisitions, education and professionalism of real estate agents, shifts in consumer behavior, homeownership, the involvement of Government on real estate and globalization.

The *Swanepoel TECHNOLOGY Report* seeks to provide information and guidance on: new technologies, the Internet, portals and aggregators, websites, video, podcasts, blogging, Social Media, social scoring, online marketing, mobile media and the paperless transaction

COMPLIMENTARY COPIES

Trends do not appear or disappear in a single year, or apply to only one year, and therefore only apply to one edition of our Reports. Trends almost always span many years, even decades, and technology often has a lasting impact for decades. Each *Swanepoel TRENDS Report* and *Swanepoel TECHNOLOGY Report* is written starting with a blank sheet of paper and is thus a totally separate and independent Report. Reports should be read together. Depending on the subject matter, a three to five year range of Reports should be read on a specific topic. Therefore free copies of all previous editions for the last three years are available on RETrends.com for your viewing and complimentary downloading.

LIMIT OF LIABILITY / DISCLAIMER OF WARRANTY

While the publisher, authors, contributors and editors have used their best efforts in preparing this Report, they make no representation or warranties with respect to the accuracy or completeness of the contents of this report and specifically disclaim any implied warranties. The advice, strategies and comments contained herein may not be suitable for your market or situation.

Although the authors and contributors may, from time-to-time, be an investor in companies mentioned in the Report, and most certainly serve as a consultant and/or advisor to numerous companies and organizations stated in the Report, the Report is written as a neutral, accurate and reasonable view of the industry and its participants. References to any companies, products, services and websites do not constitute or imply endorsement and neither is any reference or absence of reference intended to harm, place at a disadvantage or in any way affect any company or person. Information contained in this Report should not be a substitute for common sense, thorough research and competent advice.

As far as possible all statements, statistics and information included in this Report were verified with the parties mentioned or a credible source. Information is not treated casually and great pride is taken to provide accurate information. The advice, strategies and comments contained herein may not be suitable for your market or situation and readers are urged to consult proper counsel or other experts regarding any points of law, finance, technology and business before proceeding. All conclusions expressed herein are also of course subject to local, state and federal laws and regulations. Neither the publishers, authors, contributors nor editors shall be liable for any loss or any other commercial damages, including but not limited to special, incidental, consequential, or other damages.

1 The Secret to Maximizing Your Internet Presence

Blogging: The Key to Prospecting,
Networking and Building Relationships

The Secret to Maximizing Your Internet Presence

While the term "weblog"—later shortened to just "blog"—wasn't coined until the late 90s, its history began at the dawn of the Internet in the late 80s with digital communities in the form of user groups and bulletin boards. True, 20 years isn't a long history, but it's been a history filled with tremendous growth, technological advances and change.

Just do a simple Web search on "real estate blog" and Google returns over a billion results. True, not every one of those pages is a real estate blog, but this does give you some indication as to just how ubiquitous the concept of blogging has become. It has clearly survived its childhood and adolescence, and now it's moving into adulthood as we watch this excellent online platform mature.

POPULARITY OF BLOGS

The Internet ushered in a new era in which people are accustomed to having vast amounts of information readily available at their fingertips, 24 hours a day, seven days a week, from anywhere on the planet. TThis has created a vacuum into which blogging, at least in part, has risen up to help fill. The popularity and large quantity of blogs can be attributed to the following key elements:

> Just do a simple web search on "real estate blog" and Google returns over a billion results.

Ease of Use

Prior to the introduction of WordPress (wordpress.com), TypePad (typepad.com), Blogger (blogger.com) and other blogging platforms, creating a webpage typically entailed using an editor and writing HTML code. Realizing early the power of the Internet, companies developed website packages that catered to real estate professionals, allowing them to add listings and create webpages relatively easily without extensive use of HTML, CSS, PHP and other commonly used programming languages. WYSIWYG—What You See Is What You Get—editing greatly simplified the creation of pages and sites. WordPress revolutionized Internet publishing by introducing into the mix a platform that is flexible and powerful, yet simple enough for just about anyone to use.

Inexpensive Hosting

Hosting costs for a real estate blog range from free to hundreds of dollars per month. Since most blogs don't have the volume of visitor traffic necessary to require advanced hosting options or need the horsepower of expensive hosting, free is the most popular option. That alternative is typically supported by ads, while many blogs run perfectly well on hosting in the $7 - $20 per month range.

Conversation

Ideally, a blog facilitates engagement between the blog author and readers who comment on the author's posts; however, not every blog enables comments. Comments can extend discussions, build communities and enable near real-time communication and follow up.

Search Engines

Many people use the Internet to find homes and the real estate agents who sell them, the vast majority using a search engine to accomplish those tasks. While the search engines are quite secretive about the algorithms they

employ to determine Search Engine Results Placement (SERP), it is generally accepted by Search Engine Optimization (SEO) specialists that certain aspects of blogs—from their underlying code structure to the addition of regularly updated content—are helpful in achieving good search engine results.

WHAT IS A BLOG?

The simplest way to think of a blog is that it's a website where articles you write (or have written by other contributors) and other content you generate are posted and organized chronologically.

A blog is simply another form or type of website, which comes in an almost infinite array of designs and functionalities. Broken down into its simplest form, a blog is a website where entries (also known as articles, posts or even, confusingly, blogs) are arranged with the most recent post at the top of the main page and older posts at the bottom (although more sophisticated blogs allow for the presentation of this information in a variety of ways).

Many of today's real estate blogs now also incorporate an IDX (Internet Data eXchange) solution—a home search—as well as video, images, a menu structure and other components of older websites. As more and more web designers and developers

support the major blogging platforms, more functionality is being added and the distinctions between traditional websites and blogs is becoming even further blurred.

WHY SHOULD I BLOG?

To be a successful real estate agent you need clients. The average time between home purchases for the typical homeowner is seven years according to a report by the National Association of REALTORS® (NAR). If you've been a real estate agent for less than seven years, there is a reasonable chance that you've never sold a second home to a past client or, if you have, you've not done that very many times. It often takes years to generate enough business to afford the luxury of working only with past clients and their friends and family.

To connect with enough clients to make a solid, consistent living, the vast majority of agents have to prospect for or generate leads in one form or another. Whatever term you choose to use, you have to actively seek out new clients. How much prospecting you'll need to do depends on several factors, including your desired income level, your ability to convert a prospect contact into a client and the relative efficiency of your chosen prospecting method(s).

It's in that third factor—prospecting efficiency—where blogging and other online prospecting methods truly

shine. The very nature of the Internet lends itself to efficient prospecting methods. According to Internet World Stats (internetworldstats.com), 78.6 percent of the U.S. population had Internet access by December 2012. It provides you with a platform to billions of people around the globe that is open 24/7/365.

This is not to say that any and every online tool or system makes for efficient prospecting. As with virtually anything, the effectiveness and efficiency of any prospecting method—online or offline—varies

wildly and depends on many factors. Generally speaking, however, the Internet is where a lot of people are looking for homes, real estate information and agents. The simple fact that with a website you can literally prospect in your sleep demonstrates that there is remarkable potential in Internet prospecting.

NAR reported in its 2012 *Profile of Home Buyers and Sellers* that 90 percent of all homebuyers searched for homes online; Exhibit 3-4 from the Profile is excerpted on page 19. For buyers in the 25 – 44 age group, that number increased to 96 percent. Given the weight of these statistics, it seems prudent to have some sort of Internet presence.

TYPES OF BLOGS

There are three basic types of real estate websites: Lead or Prospect

Generation, Information Repository and Vanity or Electronic Business Card.

1. Lead or Prospect Generation Sites

Most agent and broker sites fall under this category. In this scenario, a site is built for the primary purpose of generating potential homebuyer or seller prospects, which the agent will then cultivate and, at some point, hopefully convert into clients.

2. Information Repository

An information repository site allows you to add content of various types in order to build a "library" of reference material that can either be discovered online by a search engine query, or sent (by a link or electronic file) as a

direct response to an inquiry made by a client or prospect. For example, you are showing your buyers homes and they ask you, "Should we get a home inspection?" Your response: "Great question! The short answer is yes, but I've written an article I can send you that will answer that exact question in detail." You can then email the client a link to the article you wrote on home inspections (or send them a PDF version of the article).

The general theory here is that you will, over time, create content that answers all of the most frequently asked questions (FAQ) your clients or prospects will likely ask. Over the long haul this saves you time as you can quickly provide answers

digitally without "recreating the wheel" every time the same question is asked. This can also position you as knowledgeable or perhaps even an expert as your library of answers grows larger and becomes more robust.

If you don't care to generate leads from your website, an information repository can be less expensive (as no IDX solution is required) and time intensive (as no lead follow up required) and still serve a very valuable purpose and promote client satisfaction. Of note, a prospect generation site can also serve as an information repository site.

3. Electronic Business Card

Some agents feel that they "have to have a website to look current." They don't really care if it generates leads, and they don't want to take the time and effort required to build up an information repository. They simply want a basic website to serve as a "digital placeholder" of sorts. While this is the simplest of all types of sites, it probably won't do anything significant in terms of revenue generation or client satisfaction.

There is no right or wrong type of website and what you choose as the ultimate purpose of your site will depend on your business, commitment, skill set and needs. Every real estate blog does, however, need a goal.

GOAL SETTING

Most real estate bloggers don't realize that having a goal and purpose for their blog is as important as deciding to create one in the first place. To have an effective blog you need to

Early Real Estate Blogs that Obtained National Notoriety

biggerpockets.com
irvinehousingblog.com
lansner.ocregister.com
locomusings.com
phoenixrealestateguy.com
miamism.com
raincityguide.com
realestatetamato.com
realcentralva.com
thehousingbubbleblog.com

SOURCE REALSURE, INC.

be SMART: Specific, Measurable, Achievable, Relevant and Time-bound. Let's explore each component in greater detail.

1. Specific
"More business" isn't specific. Everyone wants more business. More what? More clients, more money, more frequent paydays, more listings, more buyers, etc.? You need to be more precise and detailed.

2. Measurable
Many might say, "I want a good blog" or "I want a recognized/respected blog," but how do you measure "good" or "recognized?" If you can't measure something, then you can't track your performance.

3. Achievable
There is no point in setting an unachievable goal. If you do, you're just setting yourself up for failure. Saying, "I want as many RSS (Really Simple Syndication) subscribers as Chris Brogan has!"—while both specific and measurable—may not be realistically achievable.

4. Relevant
Perhaps your ultimate goal is to sell enough real estate to retire so you can sit on a beach and sip cocktails out of coconuts. Aside from that lofty goal not being Specific, it's not really relevant for a real estate blog. Ditto for "I want to write a New York Times bestseller based on my blog." A real estate blog doesn't have enough reach to make the New York Times list. You need to have a goal that is relevant to what you can do with a blog.

5. Time-bound
This one basically keeps you honest. If, for example, RSS subscribers are your goal, proclaiming, "I want 5,000 subscribers" doesn't cut it. Or "I want 100 people to register for a home search." Those would be a SMAR goal. Add the "T"—"I want 100 people to register for a home search in the next six months"—and then you have a legitimate goal. Here are some possible SMART criteria/categories to consider when creating goals for your blog:

- Home search registrations.
- Email addresses added to a newsletter distribution list.
- Email inquiries/phone calls received on home listings.
- Number of listing appointments taken.
- RSS/email subscribers.
- Page views/unique visitors.

Don't like SMART goals? DUMB goals work too: Doable, Understandable, Manageable and Beneficial. You might also think about adding an "ER" to the end of either of those acronyms: Evaluate and Re-evaluate, thus making your goals SMARTER and/or DUMBER.

BLOGGING ESSENTIALS
The following fifteen key items cover some fundamental aspects of what most successful real estate blogs include. These items won't be appropriate for every type of website, but they do provide some insight, tips and tactics that have been proven to work.

1. IDX Solution
As previously stated, the vast

Information Sources Used In Home Search By Age					
	All Buyers	18 to 24	25 to 44	45 to 64	65 or older
Internet	90%	96%	96%	90%	69%
Real Estate Agent	87%	88%	87%	87%	89%
Yard Sign	53%	45%	51%	54%	52%
Open House	45%	28%	46%	45%	41%
Print Newspaper Advertisement	27%	24%	23%	31%	34%
Home Builder	17%	18%	16%	17%	19%
Home Book or Magazine	18%	20%	16%	20%	18%
Relocation Company	4%	2%	3%	4%	2%
Television	5%	6%	5%	5%	2%
Billboard	5%	3%	5%	5%	3%

SOURCE NATIONAL ASSOCIATION OF REALTORS® - PROFILE OF HOME BUYERS AND SELLERS 2012

majority of people start looking for homes on the Internet. As such, one of the most crucial components of your lead generation website is an IDX solution. Fundamentally, it's how the Multiple Listing Service (MLS) is displayed on an agent or broker website. The site won't actually have a user-searchable MLS on it, as only paying MLS members can access the full MLS, but through the IDX, a "feed" of much of the data can be displayed on the website and be searched by visitors.

A good IDX solution will allow users to register, allowing them to save searches, get notifications when new listings meeting their criteria come on the market, share their favorite listings, etc. In most cases, when a user registers to search they are required to provide a name and an email address, and optionally a phone number. With that information you can begin to establish a rapport with them that will hopefully end in an agent/client relationship.

There are a large number of IDX providers, and cost varies by location and vendor, generally ranging from $20 – $80 per month.

With over 800 MLSs across the country, not every IDX supplier supports every MLS. Larger and more popular solutions, like Diverse Solutions (diversesolutions.com) and IDXBroker (idxbroker.com), support hundreds of MLSs. Other suppliers are more regional in focus and support a very limited number. Fees that MLSs charge agents and brokers to access the listing data also vary widely. You should be aware that some MLSs will only allow brokers (and not individual agents) to have direct IDX data feeds on their sites.

2. About Us Page

The "About" (or "About Us") page is typically the second or third most visited page on a website (after the home page and IDX pages). When a visitor clicks the "About" page they expect to be able to find out some information about you; your experience, background and customer service philosophy, etc. But since real estate is such a personal business, and clients want to connect with an agent with whom they can relate, go ahead and include a little personality. You don't need to provide intimate life details, but including a little bit about your personal life is often effective

and well received. Buying real estate is a very personal and emotional experience for most people, so give them something about you they can connect with.

Furthermore, you should provide visitors to your site with details regarding how they can reach you by phone, email and regular mail, as well as by Social Media platforms like Twitter, Facebook and LinkedIn. They should be able to select their preferred method of contacting you, as it's always best to communicate with people the way THEY want to communicate.

Here are some great resources to check out:

- Best Practices For Effective Design Of "About me" Pages—Smashing Magazine (bit.ly/Z7SFy8).

- Best About Pages (bestaboutpages.com).

- Making a Good Impression With About Us Pages—Search Engine Land (selnd.com/166tSxG).

WHAT IS IDX?

IDX, or Internet Data Exchange, also known as Broker Reciprocity, incorporates all of the policies, rules, and software that allow listings from the MLS database to be displayed on a website. The majority of real estate agents and brokers use IDX to simply display MLS listings or home search tools on their website, but as home buyers have become more Internet-savvy, IDX has become much more.

SOURCE WIKIPEDIA

3. Contact Information

A striking number of agent websites are missing a very crucial, fundamental piece of information: how to reach you. Make sure you provide this information.

4. Above the Fold

There is a saying in the newspaper industry; "above the fold." This refers to the content that is above the fold of a newspaper, which is the most readily viewable part of a traditionally folded paper and which therefore gets the most attention. On a website, above the fold refers to the content that is visible on the screen without scrolling.

Best Practice Suggestion

- Use Google Analytics (google.com/analytics) to see how much of a webpage is shown on monitors with various resolution settings. Since content above the fold is viewed more often and easier to find, it's an ideal place to put your basic contact info. As a suggestion, put at least a phone number and an email address in the header of your site.

5. Sidebar

The sidebar area of a blog is an ideal spot to put a widget with contact info or a small contact form as content in the sidebar is typically displayed on every page. Again, above the fold will help with visibility.

Wordpress Blog Statistics

SOURCE WORDPRESS

6. Contact Page

There is only so much you can squeeze into a header or a text widget. While phone and email are the primary methods of contact that most people employ, setting up a separate contact page with ALL the ways people can find you is a good idea. You can include links to social networks/profiles you use, secondary phone numbers, fax number and a business address.

7. Bottom of Posts

While the area above the fold definitely gets the most visibility, there is one important thing to remember: if a visitor scrolls down, your contact information may scroll off the screen. While the visitor could scroll back up to access the info, numerous studies have shown that visitors are easily frustrated and prone to moving on to another site if they can't easily find what they're looking for. Putting your basic contact info at the bottom of every post, or in the footer of the site, will keep it front and center at all times.

9. Call to Action

Call to Action (CTA) is probably the most powerful component of a successful prospect generation site. You want people to do something when they're on your site, something

From the Vault: Real Estate Confronts Reality (1997)

10

"The Internet is big, really big – maybe even the biggest business opportunity of the 21st Century."

that will allow at least an email address to be captured. We'll reference a number of good CTAs throughout the remainder of this chapter.

10. Home Search Registration

Most visitors to your site want to search for homes. By providing a feature-rich home IDX solution you empower them to do what they came for. "Forcing" registration for a home search, which refers to requiring users to enter some level of contact information in order to get what they want from your site, is a hotly debated topic. Opponents of forced registration feel that making a visitor enter personal data may drive them to some other site where they won't be required to register. Proponents argue that you're providing a valuable service by allowing users to search for homes on your site, and asking for fundamental contact info in return is fair and reasonable.

IDX solution providers have just recently begun to understand that in addition to providing a user-friendly, rich search experience for the consumer, they must also provide features for you. For example, the ability to control parameters around when a registration box is presented to a user is crucial for a lead generation blog. Typical parameters you can define are the number of searches made and the number of listings viewed. By adjusting the limits of these two values you can allow visitors to see a few listings before asking them to register—a compromise between having no registration and asking for it immediately. By enabling this feature you allow the visitor to see and understand what it is you're offering before you ask them to register. Once you build up enough traffic on your website, testing various registration settings to optimize registration count and quality is recommended.

11. FAQs

Having an FAQ section on your site is a great CTA and an excellent way to begin engaging with potential homebuyers and sellers.

Best Practice Suggestion

- When a client asks you a question, answer the question by creating a blog post and you can then email the questioner a link to the post and a library of content will be built on the site at the same time.

12. Subscribe to Newsletter/RSS Feeds

Email marketing is an often-neglected avenue for reaching out and maintaining top-of-mind awareness with current, past and prospective clients. Placing a CTA on your website to sign up for your newsletter can add names to your marketing database. RSS is another avenue that allows WordPress posts to be sent to a subscriber's feed reader. Here are some great resources about this topic:

- How I use Email Newsletters to Drive Traffic and Make Money (bit.ly/Wt9vcj)

- Why Your Blog Should Have an Email Newsletter (bit.ly/12rLwgj).

- You Need Your Own Email Newsletter (bit.ly/102qG1L).

- A Copywriter's Tips: How To Write Lean Email Copy (bit.ly/ZmauaS).

- What is RSS? (bit.ly/Zmazev).

13. Home Valuation

Homebuyers go to the Internet to search for homes, and home sellers go there to find out how much their homes are worth. Offering a Comparative Market Analysis (CMA) is a great way to initiate contact as well as offer something of value to your site visitors.

Best Practice Suggestion

- Don't try to build a form for someone to complete that provides all the answers you need to construct a CMA;

visitors don't like to fill out long complicated forms. Instead, place a button or link in a prominent spot on your webpages that goes to a short contact form that the user can complete (providing name, email address and phone number). Then you can reach out to them personally to collect the info you need to prepare the CMA.

Best Practice Suggestion

- Don't use language like "FREE CMA!" in your call to action. While it's true that we all know what CMA means, most consumers don't. Try language like, "What is my home worth?" or "Free Home Valuation." Use language consumers understand and are searching with.

14. Local Market Statistics

Homebuyers and sellers alike are interested in what's happening in the local real estate market. Offering a "Free Market Report" or "Free Market Analysis" is an excellent CTA. Many MLSs offer ways to compile market statistics and information and Realtors Property Resource (RPR; narrpr.com), if it's available in your area, offers free market tools and

reports. In addition, there are several additional market stats/analysis options available from third-party vendors that provide ready-to-use stats.

15. Content

"Content is King." Content is what search engines see and love; but not just any old content. What search engines and your visitors like to see is original, fresh and unique content. This is such an important part of blogging that we're going to dedicate the whole next section to this vitally important topic.

CONTENT
Overview

It's important to note that you don't have to write like Hemingway or Faulkner. It does help, however, to spell properly and have reasonable sentence structure. It's also important to point out that content is not just the written word. Content can also be pictures, videos, surveys, polls, etc.—anything that can go on a webpage is considered content. You don't (and ideally shouldn't) limit yourself to just writing articles. A combination of content types helps make your blog

more interesting to visitors as well as more fun and exciting to produce.

One of the benefits of creating content for a real estate site is that you can write about virtually anything and connect it to real estate (not all content needs to be directly related to real estate). Is a new restaurant opening in an area where you sell homes? Stop by for lunch and write a review or interview the owner on video and embed that video in your blog. Post a local events calendar. Write posts about local neighborhoods. The options are almost infinite.

Specific Copy

Don't just post a chart of the number of homes listed for sale. Post the chart with your explanation of what home inventory means, and the effects of

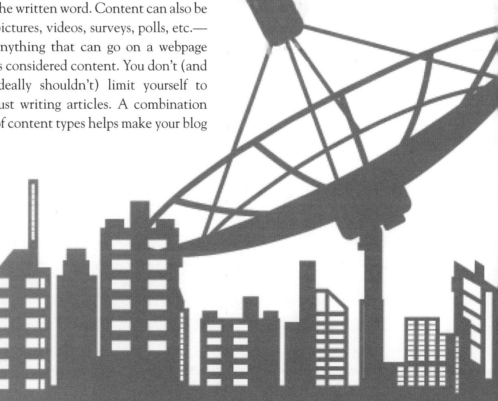

changing inventory levels. It's your opinion and analysis of the data that will set you apart from everyone else that just posts a chart.

Where applicable to your specific content, and if your IDX search solution supports it, embed listings from the area about which you're creating that content. Some IDX providers have a feature called a "short code" that will display current neighborhood listings automatically. Even if someone visits your post weeks or months after you originally created it, they will still see fresh content detailing currently active homes for sale because of the way that data refreshes automatically.

Again, always remember this crucial point: content doesn't have to be all about real estate. It's acceptable, and often preferable, to include some personal content. Potential homebuyers and sellers connect with agents they want to work with for many reasons. Write about your hobbies, your kids' activities, your vacation, etc. That gets "you the person" out there for others to see, and lets potential clients connect with you on a deeper and more personal level.

Other Applications for Copy

If you generate enough quality material of similar content, you can always consider compiling the articles into a white paper or eBook and offering that as an inducement to sign up for your newsletter, or as a stand-alone product. These compilations can make compelling CTAs:

- First-time Homebuyer Tips.
- Free eBook — Financing a New Home.
- Info for Canadians on Buying U.S. Property.
- A summary of your FAQ.

Make sure that your white papers and eBooks are available in PDF format so they are cross-platform compatible and a user doesn't need a specific piece of software to open them.

Where to Get Ideas

One of the best places to get ideas for content is in your "sent" email folder. Agents are always answering questions from clients and prospects. Scroll through your old emails and look for questions you've been asked. You'll likely already have the answers to many in your sent folder. Questions and answers make great content pages.

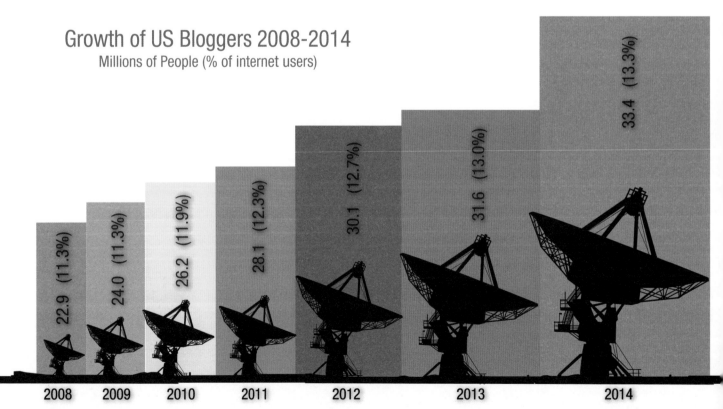

Growth of US Bloggers 2008-2014
Millions of People (% of internet users)

22.9 (11.3%) — 2008
24.0 (11.3%) — 2009
26.2 (11.9%) — 2010
28.1 (12.3%) — 2011
30.1 (12.7%) — 2012
31.6 (13.0%) — 2013
33.4 (13.3%) — 2014

SOURCE EMARKETER

Related to the sent email folder idea is this: consider questions you regularly get from buyers and sellers you're working with. With very little thought and effort you can probably write down dozens of questions you get from buyers and sellers on a regular basis. Any question about the home buying/selling process can become content for your website.

Sources for Copy

Another solid source of content ideas is Internet forums. There are several real estate-related Internet forums, groups and message boards where buyers and sellers regularly pose questions to real estate professionals and the general public. These sites are content gold mines. Write a blog post answering a question about which you're knowledgeable and then post a link to that answer in the forum. Be sure you check forum posting rules first, as some don't allow linking back to other sites, but you can certainly still use the questions as topics for posts on your site. Here are some places to look:

- Zillow Advice (zillow. com/advice) is a Q &A forum where real estate buyers, sellers, investors and agents pose and respond to questions. At the time of this writing there were over 400,000 postings in the Zillow Advice area.

- Trulia Voices (trulia.com/ voices) is one of the largest real estate Q&A forums on the Internet. At the time of this writing it had almost 500,000 postings. Some

questions are very specific to a location while others are more general in nature.

- City Data (citydata.com) has hundreds, if not thousands, of city-specific forums as well as a dedicated real estate forum.

- The Real Estate Forum (realestateforum.com) contains thousands of threads and content ideas; see the "Ask a Realtor" section.

When all else fails, go to Google and search for terms like "real estate blog topics" or "what to write about on a real estate blog." There are lists of blog topic ideas posted all over the Internet.

Curating Content

A fairly new catchphrase that's being tossed about a lot these days is "content curation." In its simplest form, this refers to the collection and sharing of the most interesting things being said about a particular subject. Content curation is NOT stealing other people's work and repurposing it for your own good or as your own. Some people try curating content because they think it will be easier than creating their own original content. Many think, "I'll just throw together a few links, put them in a blog post and I'm done for the day." Unfortunately, it's not that easy. Done well, content curation can be a very powerful tactic for disseminating information and positioning yourself

> **Call to Action is probably the most powerful component of a successful prospect generation site.**

as a topic expert. Here are some articles that offer more insight:

- Content Curation Primer (bit.ly/12rJbSE).

- Content Curation Guide for SEO – What, How, Why (mz.cm/WMO46u).

- Five Tips for Great Content Curation (on.mash.to/Wt83XB).

Copyright and Plagiarism

It's illegal to copy and paste almost anything you see on the Internet. And just because you can copy something doesn't make it right. Doing that without attribution is not only plagiarism; it can be a violation of Federal copyright law.

Fair Use

"Fair use" in copyright law allows you to use small portions of an original work if properly attributed. On the Internet "proper attribution" typically consists of a link to the original source. Fair use is not well defined but, generally speaking, it's acceptable to copy and paste a few sentences or a short paragraph of an

WHAT IS FAIR USE?

Fair Use is a legal doctrine which states that portions of copyrighted materials may be used without permission of the copyright owner provided the use is fair and reasonable, does not substantially impair the value of the materials, and does not curtail the profits reasonably expected by the owner.

original work into your content as long as proper credit is given to the author. The bottom line: use extreme caution when copying original work into a piece of content you're producing. Here are some additional Copyright resources you should review:

- U.S. Copyright Office – Fair Use (copyright.gov/fls/fl102. html).

- U.S. Copyright Office – Copyright Basics (copyright. gov/circs/circ01.pdf).

- Plagiarism and the Internet (plagiarism.org).

- PlagiarismToday (plagiarismtoday.com).

ADVANTAGES AND DISADVANTAGES

Jay Thompson, author of The Phoenix Real Estate Guy blog (see case study below), has tracked more than 600 real estate blogs over the last seven years. According to Thompson, fully two-thirds of those blogs are no longer active. Why have so many blogs faded away over time? There are two likely reasons: the blogger's goals weren't met and/or the blogger simply fell victim to the grind of the long-term effort.

Blogging is hard work. To be successful, a blog needs to be continuously updated and modified. Content must be generated and calls to action created, tested and refined. Software needs to be updated. Websites break and need to be fixed and they get hacked and need to be secured. There are times when it seems like the work never ends.

It also takes significant time for a blog to gain readership and begin generating prospects. Then those prospects you work so hard to create have to be contacted, nurtured and developed. Many real estate bloggers report that their blogs didn't start becoming effective until a year or more after they were founded. It takes significant perseverance to stick with something for a year, hoping for a payoff.

Advantages of Blogging
- Builds Internet presence.
- Builds top-of-mind awareness.
- Creates a resource library.
- Refines and sharpens writing and communication skills.
- Displays knowledge and

expertise.
- Provides potential clients with a means to get to know you.
- Researching blog posts increases personal knowledge.
- Low out of pocket cost.

Disadvantages of Blogging
- Takes time and effort to write posts.
- Requires some level of technical aptitude.
- Potentially surfaces legal/liability concerns.
- Almost always involves personal writing, which some find difficult.
- Blog sites require upkeep and maintenance.
- Takes time to develop an audience.
- Takes time to nurture leads.
- Requires tenacity, perseverance and commitment.

CASE STUDY
As Jay Thompson has tracked so many blogs we thought he would be

an ideal case study for this chapter. Jay's blog (phoenixrealestateguy. com) is also a former winner of Inman News' "Most Innovative Blog" award. Prior to taking his current position at Zillow (he's now their Director of Industry Outreach & Social Media), he told us that his blog was the central hub of all his business. He directed everything (his neighborhood websites, his tweets, his Facebook posts, etc.) back to the blog, and for the following reasons:

- It's easier to update than his traditional website. Using the web to create business is "all about content creation," and the blog is the easiest place to do that.

- He enjoys writing and the blog is the most natural place to do that. He started writing one post per week, but he said that he didn't start seeing results until he focused on publishing posts with much greater frequency, which he did for two to three years to get his visitor traffic up to its peak.

- Blog posts have "legs" that other things don't. That is, he's picked up clients from blog posts he wrote three or four years ago, and he doesn't believe that this "longevity" aspect is applicable to tweets or Facebook posts.

- Thompson used to get approximately 80 percent of his business from his blog. He admits, however, that growth has been a "slow and steady climb" and that calculating your return on investment (ROI) is very hard to do.

- He has created web leads "in the thousands" for his agents from his various web activities, with about 90 percent of those leads coming from the blog.

SUMMARY

Blogging isn't for everyone. At a minimum, you need to be able to write ideally at least three times a week. You could eschew writing altogether and develop a video or photo blog, but those types also require a significant investment of time and effort. However, if you'll make the effort you will find a blog both personally and professionally rewarding and satisfying; educating the public, providing a voice, expressing your opinions and generating business are all worthwhile endeavors.

The immediate future of blogging is very promising. Given the general public's thirst for information, and the immediate access to that information that the Internet provides, it's hard to imagine that blogs will ever completely go away. They will morph and change over time as design trends and technologies change. Current design trends are calling for responsive themes (webpages that expand and contract perfectly to match the size of the applicable user's display screen), minimal design and well-structured menu systems. Agents are putting more thought into the real goals of their blogs and methods to assure those goals are met. At the other end of the opinion spectrum, some have postulated that the growth of Social Media spells death for blogs.

It's critical to understand that blogging can take a considerable amount of time and effort. In evaluating whether or not to undertake blogging you should consider the goal you set for your blog and weigh the impact of achieving that goal against the time commitment required. Giving up an existing, effective lead generation program in order to free up time to blog probably doesn't make sense. While it can be difficult to correlate single real estate transactions to specific blogging efforts, you must attempt to determine what the ROI is for your efforts.

What it all boils down to is this: many homebuyers begin their home search on the Internet and therefore it's prudent to consider and evaluate an "Internet presence" strategy. With the ease of use, large user community, low hard dollar cost and high potential for effectiveness, blogging can be one of the most effective strategies for increasing Internet presence and generating new leads.

Guidelines to Expand Your Online Real Estate Niche

Podcasting: An Opportunity of Episodic Nature

Expanding Your Online Real Estate Niche

A podcast is a type of digital media, normally serialized in nature, which is consumed by users via web syndication or by streaming to a computer or mobile device. The word "podcast" is a derivative of the words "iPod" and "broadcast," as podcasts are increasingly being consumed on portable media players like the iPod. So a podcast is basically a recording of some variety that can be an audio or video recording of almost any length. It can be edited or unedited, streamed live or recorded and listened to at a later time. It is usually subscription-based and serial in nature, similar to a TV series.

Podcasting dates back to the 80s, before the emergence of the World Wide Web. At that time several different types of audio and recording formats were used, but with the growth of the Internet the distribution of content was standardized to RSS news feeds. A further advancement in 2000 enabled the downloading of music and audio files on the fly, moving podcasting to a new level. That led to an explosion in 2005 when Apple (apple.com) released a version of iTunes that contained native support for podcasts, allowing people to subscribe to various podcasts through the iTunes Music Store (apple.com/itunes) and download them directly into their iPods. This opened the door to the mass market and podcasting went mainstream. Like any other digital realm, podcasting is constantly in a state of flux and innovation.

Per PodcastAlley.com, approximately 92,000 podcasts are produced annually, and according to Edison Research's Podcast Consumer 2012 Report (edisonresearch.com), 45 percent of Americans over the age of 12 have heard of a podcast and 29 percent have actually listened to one. The incredible surge in the use of notebook and tablet devices dovetails nicely with podcast consumption, with up to 50 percent of all podcasts currently being listened to or watched on mobile phones or tablets.

The number of podcasts increased by roughly 31 percent between 2009 and 2011 (see graphic). And while the growth rate from 2011 to now has been somewhat flat, other statistics, factors and trends indicate that the future of podcasting may actually be brighter than the recent rate of growth might lead you to believe (more later).

It's also important to note that there is far less competition

Total Number of Podcasts

2011 — 91,659

2010 — 89,455

2009 — 69,860

SOURCE PODCASTALLEY.COM

in podcasting than in other digital domains. For example, it's estimated that there are over 180 million unique blogs and "tens of millions" of YouTube channels (that's as specific as YouTube will state publicly). But with so few podcasts being created, this illustrates the significant opportunity for those who would embrace podcasting in general and real estate podcasting in particular.

PODCASTING IN 2013

The following findings were reported in the Podcast Consumer 2012 Report, published by Edison Research in May 2012:

- 29 percent of Americans listened to a podcast, representing a 264 percent increase from 2006 (see graphic).

- Roughly one in six Americans have listened to an audio podcast or viewed a video podcast in the past month.

- Half of podcast consumers are between the ages of 12 and 34.

- Four in ten podcast consumers have a household income of at least $75,000.

- About one in five Smartphone users are podcast consumers.

- Podcast consumers are more likely to use social networks, especially Facebook (see graphic Page 32).

- Podcast consumers are heavy YouTube users.

Here are our observations from these key statistics:

- Podcasting continues to be an effective way to reach affluent consumers, making it perfect for real estate.

- Smartphone ownership is exploding and there seems to be a strong correlation between Smartphone ownership and podcast consumption; ergo, more Smartphones should equate to more demand for podcasts.

- The explosion of Smartphone ownership also suggests a likely rise in "watch/listen on demand" consumption, as opposed to "download and watch/listen" consumption, which is the more typical form of consumption on a computer.

- Podcast users love Facebook and video, so be sure that Facebook and YouTube are part of your syndication and distribution strategy.

Also worth noting is the fact that traditional radio stations and television outlets are increasing the amount of podcasts they produce. More than one-third of radio outlets offered podcasts in 2011, up from 23 percent in 2010 according to Robert Papper, professor of journalism at Hofstra University. The number of television stations that made podcasts available grew to 14 percent, up from 10 percent over that same time period. That's because, according to Edison's research, 41 percent of podcast consumers watch TV on their computers, 14 percent on their tablets and 13 percent on their Smartphones. Everything just seems to be migrating more and more

% Who Have Ever Listened To A Podcast

% of American Population

06: 11
07: 13
08: 18
09: 22
10: 23
11: 25
12: 29

SOURCE EDISON RESEARCH

to Mobile (Read more on Mobile and the Paperless Agent in Chapters 9 and 10, respectively).

While surveys such as those conducted by Edison Research show promising numbers in terms of increased usage, podcasting still remains a niche market, and a fragmented one at that. It is truly still in its infancy. While the creators and consumers of this technology remain smaller in number compared to a platform such as Facebook, those who listen to and create podcasts do so avidly. Podcasting is still in the "pre-critical mass" stage, but when it does break that threshold the market for quality content may rise dramatically.

PODCAST DIRECTORIES

There are a variety of podcast directories in the fields of business, technology, education, comedy and politics. While some provide resources for hosting and promoting podcasts, others are great places to find podcasts worth checking out. One such example can be found at bit.ly/Z7RjUg.

If you aren't sure where to begin listening to podcasts, a good starting point is to review which ones were nominated for and/or won national awards relating to podcasting. Those awards are announced annually, and you can see the nominees in each category at podcastawards.com. In addition, two podcasting reference websites worth investigating are Podcasts.com and Podcast.com.

Podcasts.com is a good site for both creators and consumers. As a creator you can manage episodes on their backend, view reports on how many downloads each episode has had and set up premium subscriptions. They also offer a search engine optimized podcast directory and they allow you to submit your podcast's RSS feed to be listed in that directory for free. Podcast.com offers a podcast database divided into different subjects, making it easy to search, explore and listen.

CASE STUDIES

First, we'll take a look at how Adam Carolla, a radio disc jockey in California, turned a podcast into a media empire worth millions, and then we'll move on to two examples from within the real estate industry.

The World's Most Downloaded Podcast

According to the Guinness Book of World Records the most downloaded podcast belongs to Adam Carolla, host of the Adam Carolla Show (adamcarolla.com). The 48-year-old comedian and actor got his start as a radio personality in Los Angeles. From 1995-2005 he co-hosted a radio call-in program called Loveline with Dr. Drew Pinksky (now on HLN TV network) and he hosted a television version of the show on MTV for four years, from 1996-2000.

Active in the entertainment industry with radio and TV projects, Carolla started podcasting the Adam Carolla Show in February 2009, from his garage via his own website, the day after he was fired from his radio show in Los Angeles. His 90-minute show, which he produces daily, has evolved

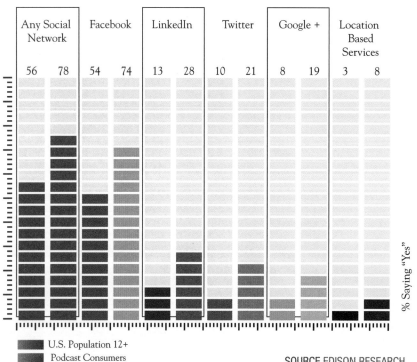

Podcast Consumers Are More Likely To Use Social Networks

Any Social Network		Facebook		LinkedIn		Twitter		Google +		Location Based Services	
56	78	54	74	13	28	10	21	8	19	3	8

% Saying "Yes"

■ U.S. Population 12+
■ Podcast Consumers

SOURCE EDISON RESEARCH

since its inception, but essentially involves Carolla interviewing a guest and providing commentary on daily news.

His first episode was downloaded 250,000 times, with a total of 1.6

by Michael McClure of Plymouth, Michigan). Both podcasts use Blog Talk Radio (blogtalkradio.com) to do live broadcasts of " Internet radio" shows that are instantly converted into podcasts, which can be found

- Mitchell's guests have ranged from prominent thought leaders inside the real estate space to a number of people from other industries with perspectives Mitchell felt

blogtalkradio℠

million downloads in the first week. Within nine months he was generating income from the podcasts by announcing ad spots at the end of episodes. In 2009 his show was named iTunes Podcast of the Year, and in 2011 he had the most downloaded podcast in the world, with over one million unique downloads from March 2009 to March 2011. According to CelebrityNetWorth. com, Carolla now has an estimated net worth of $15 million.

While it's true that Carolla was a celebrity before he started podcasting (albeit some might argue a minor one), you may be wondering what this has to do with possibly creating a podcast to augment your real estate business. His success and our lesson lie in effectively implementing the basic rules of podcasting. Simply put, he provides unique quality content on a consistent basis. And that can be done by anyone, in any industry, including real estate.

Real Estate Case Studies
Two case studies of successful podcasts in the real estate space are Agent Caffeine (created by Kelly Mitchell of Honolulu, Hawaii) and Raise the Bar Radio (created

on iTunes (Mitchell is currently in the process of transitioning to a new platform). Both podcasts average weekly listens in the thousands and both have individual episodes that have been listened to over 10,000 times.

Agent Caffeine
Mitchell began podcasting in early 2011 and launched Agent Caffeine (blogtalkradio.com/search/ agent-caffeine) in February 2012. Here are some highlights concerning her show:

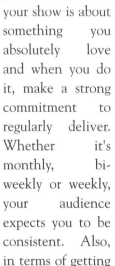

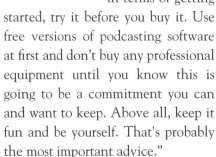
IT'S ALL ABOUT THE BUZZ

- Mitchell has a background in acting and improv.

- The objective of the show is to "give people front row seats to hear the thought leaders inside and outside the industry."

- In her first podcasting experience she hosted 35 shows.

- She has hosted 44 episodes of her current show through December 2012.

would have value to those inside real estate (e.g., Darren Rowse of Copyblogger).

Mitchell's advice to aspiring podcasters: "Get solidly into the 'why' of doing this. Making more money or getting more 'leads' is never the way to begin. If you have passion and purpose behind your 'why,' doing the shows is inspiring. Make sure your show is about something you absolutely love and when you do it, make a strong commitment to regularly deliver. Whether it's monthly, bi-weekly or weekly, your audience expects you to be consistent. Also, in terms of getting started, try it before you buy it. Use free versions of podcasting software at first and don't buy any professional equipment until you know this is going to be a commitment you can and want to keep. Above all, keep it fun and be yourself. That's probably the most important advice."

Raise the Bar Radio

McClure began Raise the Bar Radio Show (blogtalkradio.com/raisethebar) in February 2010. Here are some highlights about his show:

- McClure has a background in improv, standup comedy and public speaking.

- The objective of his show is "to have conversations around topics that in some way relate to increasing the level of professionalism in real estate."

- The show is currently in its third season, and McClure is approaching his 50th recorded episode.

- McClure's guests have been prominent thought leaders from inside real estate, along with periodic notable guests from outside the industry (e.g., Socialnomics author Erik Qualman).

McClure's advice to aspiring podcasters: "If I were going to do a podcast as an agent, I'd focus on 'local' (or probably even hyper-local) content and start to engage with local VIPs and influencers. I would create shows around local issues, local people, local places and other local

points of interest. Probably the best piece of advice I could give anyone would be this: don't start podcasting unless you are confident you can 'run the marathon' that it takes to be successful in this space. You won't have an audience immediately. It WILL take time to build, and you WILL be discouraged from time-to-time. So, if you have any doubts about your ability to hang with it when things don't seem like they're working, I would seriously caution you. You must have passion, tenacity and perseverance to have success with podcasting."

Now that we've examined a few case studies let's move on to the next logical question.

WHERE TO BEGIN

The primary reason to start your own podcasting show is to attract more clients and create more awareness about you and your real estate business. Creating podcasts can enable you to expand your sphere of influence, connect with new resources and expand your referral network. Today's real estate agent needs to home in on their specific niche, which is usually the neighborhood/market they know best, or a specific segment of the market, e.g. first time home buyers, condos, luxury properties, etc. Creating podcasts on a consistent basis offers you an opportunity to create regular content in a relatively uncrowded realm and to expand your visibility and profile to potential clients.

Characteristics to Succeed

This process begins with honest self-assessment. Here are some

characteristics we think are important for you to posses to increase your chances for success in the world of podcasting:

1. A Desire to Learn New Things

There is always a learning curve involved in mastering a new technology. To excel at podcasting, you're probably going to have to learn a few new things from a tech perspective. While some methods of podcasting are easier than others, not everyone is "tech savvy" and, for the wrong person, this can be a real waste of time. Be honest with yourself about where you fit into the tech savvy spectrum.

2. Be Conservative in Your Approach

Don't announce that you'll be releasing weekly podcasts if you only have time for monthly shows. Be conservative in how you communicate with your audience; consistency is key. You can always scale up—start monthly and increase to weekly, or start weekly and increase to twice weekly—but if you "over-promise" and "under-deliver," by not doing as much as you said you would, your audience will tend to lose respect for you.

3. Have a Real Passion for Podcasting

Your audience will be able to tell if your heart isn't in it. Experience shows that without a real passion for the things you do you probably won't survive the long haul, which leads to our last point...

4. Be Willing to "Run the Marathon"

Everything that involves building an audience takes time; often a long time. You should prepare yourself psychologically to run a marathon, not a sprint. If you're going to be easily discouraged, you'll probably give up before you achieve any meaningful level of success. You must be willing to go into podcasting with

- Which people can help you get the message out and complement your show as co-host(s) and or guest(s).

- When your show will be aired.

overall objective for the show (e.g., serious, lively, exciting, etc.), and use that theme music consistently. You can search for and purchase music on a variety of sites,

---

Podcasting is still in the "pre-critical mass" stage, but when it does break that threshold the market for quality content may rise dramatically.

---

the knowledge that it will likely take you a year or more to begin to build a real audience. You must have this long-range focus and mentality.

CREATING YOUR SHOW

1. Planning
Before you hit the record button you need to create a game plan. Planning your podcast involves strategy and thoughtfulness. With that in mind, you'll need to determine:

- Your audience.

- Your technological platform.

- The kind of equipment you'll use.

- The kinds of podcast you're going to do, e.g., news, information, interviews or something else.

- Your demographic target.

- The goals of the show.

- The "value" you're going to provide to your target audience.

- How you're going to convey your objective to your target audience.

- How often you'll do your show.

- Whether your show will be live or pre-recorded.

- Whether your show will be video or audio.

2. Preparation
Preparing for your show is the single most important thing you can do to ensure a great broadcast. Investing in pre-planning now will pay off in success later. Podcasts are linear, and having an introduction, middle and a close are important aspects of a typical show's format. Setting up a consistent flow, or "running order," is important so that your audience knows what to expect and what to anticipate. Also, consider having a very specific topical focus because there is a potential audience for almost every topic.

3. Outlining the Format
Here is an example of an outline for a typical show:

- Theme music (10 to 15 seconds): Pick music that matches the mood of your

like Pond5 (pond5.com).

- Introduction (one to two minutes): Provide a warm welcome to your audience, state the name of your show, introduce yourself briefly and share an overview of the show's guest, topic or theme.

- Coming events (one to two minutes): Announce future shows that you have scheduled and provide a brief overview of the next one or two shows.

- In the news (three to five minutes): If you're doing a show that involves coverage of current events (what's happened in your market since the last show, etc.), we

---

suggest that you cover that part before you interview your primary guest.

- Introduce your guest (one to two minutes): Provide a thumbnail sketch of your guest and why you selected them to appear on the show.

- Interview your guest for the remainder of time except for the short list of "wrap up" items that follow your interview. Obviously, this is where you will spend the vast majority of the show's time.

- Show wrap-up (one minute): Provide a quick synopsis of

and remind them of the date, time and special guest of your next show. This will help build momentum for your next show.

While you probably shouldn't script your entire show—it will sound stilted and unnatural if you do—you may want to outline a series of talking points before each episode as prompters while you're recording.

4. Creating an Editorial Calendar

You should have an editorial calendar to help keep you focused, ensure that you're lining up enough guests in a timely fashion and creating enough quality content to keep your podcast

with real value.

Here are a few examples of content:

- The most pressing issues facing your local real estate market.

- How a particular piece of legislation may affect the local construction industry.

- How a proposed new road or factory may affect nearby property values.

- The potential impact of changes to property taxes or other real estate related issues being proposed by

---

When you get to the point where your listeners view your content as "need to have"—as opposed to "nice to have"—you know you're creating a great podcast with real value

---

the highlights of the show just concluded, thank your guest for appearing and ask them for any final thoughts. Be sure to tell them how much time they have available to comment, because our experience is that guests will tend to be long-winded at this point.

- Guest closing statement (one minute): Your guest's final thoughts.

- Closing/announcement of your next show's topics/ guests (30 seconds): Thank your audience for listening

on track and on objective. Whatever your objectives, let your editorial calendar be your guide and reference it constantly. It is the blueprint and the lifeblood of your podcasting world.

5. Managing the Content

Providing unique quality content on a consistent basis is critical. The goal is to showcase your unique insight and knowledge. Not only that, you must focus on providing value—REAL value. When you get to the point where your listeners view your content as "need to have"— as opposed to "nice to have"—you know you're creating a great podcast

local government.

- The impact of changes to local building codes.

- Things that are working to get homes sold more quickly and at higher prices.

- How to navigate the home loan process.

- The steps involved in the home buying process.

- The steps involved in the home selling process.

Business leaders and subject matter experts from your geographic area

From the Vault: Real Estate Confronts Reality (1997)

"An increasing number of non-traditional players are becoming involved with or evaluating their involvement in the home buying process. This dictates that real estate practitioners shouldn't expect traditional solutions or approaches to continue to be the only way."

are excellent interview candidates, because they can offer insight and knowledge about issues close to home. For example, you might consider doing a podcast along the lines of the blog created by Dale Chumbley, the creator of clarkcountyrealestateguide.com. Chumbley became well known in the real estate industry a few years ago by showcasing his home community of Vancouver, Washington. More specifically, he set out to create a large body of content about his town, and accordingly created videos and blog posts about local people, places and things of interest. As a result, he significantly expanded his visibility and, in the process, became a national icon in the eyes of many by exemplifying how targeted content could be used to build a large local presence, and then how that local presence could be leveraged to build a bigger real estate business.

This same concept can be readily applied to podcasting. You can translate blog success like Chumbley's into podcast success by having conversations that matter to people in your town, your neighborhood, your community, etc. When you get stuck, just take a step back and think about the topics and issues that are of interest to you and your clientele. Given how complex and dynamic real estate is, there are always new

issues arising that can be suitable podcast topics.

6. Podcast Length

When determining length you should also determine what you have to say. You can always start short (say, two to 10 minutes) and expand in length, rather than ramble on for 30 minutes and bore your listeners. On the other hand, some people are naturals at podcasting and can easily carry a 60 or 90-minute show right out of the gate. For example, both Mitchell and McClure have done 60-minute live shows from day one, and both have indicated that to do anything shorter than that would feel rushed or incomplete to them. It really just depends on you and your specific skill set.

7. Podcast Name

What to call your podcasts? Select a name that people will associate with you that will expand your brand. Keep it short, professional and simple like the following examples:

- West Palm Beach Real Estate Show.

- San Diego Property Update.

- Las Vegas Condo News.

- The Murphy Team Real Estate Report.

- Portland Real Estate News.

You get the idea. Just remember to use a name that accurately conveys the real core and purpose of your podcast.

8. Booking Guests

In the beginning, when you don't have a track record, it can be relatively difficult to get guests on your podcast. To help overcome that challenge, and in order to make your guests more comfortable and more likely to accept your invitation to appear on your show, share with them ahead of time your format, your interview style, the proposed running order or agenda and what is expected of them. As your audience grows, and assuming you have some level of success, it will become easier to schedule guests as people become more aware of your show and as you create a track record of consistency and listenership.

9. Promotion

During the course of your podcast don't forget to promote your next episode. Provide a teaser of an

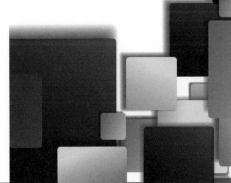

upcoming topic that will make listeners look forward to listening to your next show. And don't assume people will automatically find your podcast on the Internet. Use Social Media networks such as Twitter, Google+ and Facebook as promotional engines. Promoting through Social Media provides a great way to diversify your online reach and bring new people into your audience.

10. Resources

There are a couple of different ways to get started in podcasting, and one is to use a free platform resource where everything is basically already done for you. The other is to use your own website domain and a WordPress blog. This requires more work but it will give you more autonomy. Let's first look at the free options.

Two of the better-known free platform resources are Blog Talk Radio and TalkShoe (talkshoe.com). These online platforms make it easy for you to set up a podcast to test the waters without a lot of special equipment; they are virtually plug and play. In fact, Blog Talk Radio does everything from recording your show to scheduling and promoting it, as well as providing you and your potential listeners with a way to easily

download your recordings.

A free version of Blog Talk Radio is available, so you can start podcasting with virtually no investment. All you need is a telephone, a computer and an Internet connection. However, there are a few downsides to consider. For instance, the production capabilities are limited and bear in mind that you will always be at the mercy of these platforms. You will build your audience with them as they help you with promotion but they (potentially) make money off of your show while you get close to nothing, at least from a monetary perspective. Just remember, it's difficult to switch platforms and this will become an issue if you want to grow or take your podcast to the next level. You have to be careful about changing platforms over time as your audience will become used to how and in what manner you deliver your program. Switching platforms may cause you to lose listeners/viewers but, on the other hand, these free platforms are a great short-term way to try out podcasting and see if it's right for you.

YOUR OWN MEDIA COMPANY
The First Step

If you want to become your own media company you need to at least start out with your own domain, web hosting and WordPress site. This approach gives you more autonomy and flexibility without being held hostage to a particular platform. The best advice is to set up your platform so that you have control and ownership of all the assets and resources.

However, this approach requires a higher degree of technical skill. If you already own your own website, are familiar with web hosting and know how to use WordPress effectively then you may be ready for this option. Blubrry (blubrry.com) and Libsyn (libsyn.com) could be great resources for you. Both are media hosting companies that enable you to own your content and transfer it to a new site when you wish. Blubrry offers a variety of media services, including a plug-in that enables people to download podcasts directly from your blog. The site also offers detailed demographic and geographic information. Libsyn (short for Liberated Syndication) also works well for both novice and professional podcasters. If you don't have your own website yet, companies like Squarespace (squarespace.com) offer web hosting, mobile apps and a variety of technical assistance to get you started.

If you're unfamiliar with recording software, Audacity (audacity.sourceforge.net) is a great free resource. The award-winning website provides free, open-source software for recording and editing audio for both Macs and PCs.

Equipment

When just starting out, it's best to start simple, find out what works best for you and build upon the basics as you move forward. You can start with a computer, an Internet connection and a microphone. Generally speaking, if you want a quality microphone there are two types that will get the job done: dynamic and condenser.

Dynamic microphones are by far the easiest to work with. You can get them with a USB extension, meaning they can be plugged directly into your computer and they don't require an external power source. You can find a basic entry-level USB dynamic headset with a noise cancellation feature for under $100 at Plantronics (plantronics.com). A quick Google search will provide the latest sale prices at a variety of retailers that sell the dynamic type.

The other type that works well for podcasting is a condenser microphone. This type usually requires an external mixer or a pre-amp and a power source. They also require XLR connectors because they don't plug directly into your computer. Condenser microphones have a broader range of sound and more depth, but they are also much more complicated to set up and are best suited for a semi-permanent installation. They tend to be more expensive and can range in price from $200 - $2,500.

How do you decide which to use? Dynamic microphones have less range but are less fragile and great for on location recordings. They are easy to pick up and take on the road and are geared more toward entry-level podcasters. On the other hand, Condenser microphones are more appropriate for a home recording studio. It just depends on your situation and your long-term ambitions with your podcast.

You may also want to invest in headphones, microphone stands and other equipment as your podcasting

prowess grows. Just remember, it's simpler and easier to start small and expand rather than rush and buy a lot of expensive equipment.

Adding Music

You may find yourself wanting to use music and other resources in your podcast. In addition to Pond5, Podsafe Music Network (music.podshow. com) provides a wealth of music and also web hosting. The Association of Music Podcasting (musicpodcasting. org) is another great resource that provides podcasters with independent new music. As long as you don't make money from the podcasts, the agreements are already in place for music and other resources.

Additional Resources

Here are some other resources you should consider:

- **Podcast 411** (podcast411. com) provides everything you need to know about podcasting, from setup to software to finding jobs as a podcaster. Whether you have a Mac or a PC, their podcasting 101 tutorial will take you step-by-step through the entire process of creating your first podcast.

- **Ipodder** (ipodder.org) is a peer-reviewed podcast site that offers a decentralized directory of podcast feeds. The site provides information on how to record, publish and promote a podcast.

- **How To Podcast** (how-to-podcast-tutorial.com) covers all the basics for both novice

and more experienced podcasters. It also provides tips on improving audio capability and monetizing your podcasts.

- **iTunes** (apple.com/itunes/podcasts) has great information on podcasts as well, both from a consumption and a creation perspective.

SUMMARY

While creating a podcast is certainly not as easy as posting on Facebook or Twitter, podcasting doesn't require an immense amount of technical skill or knowledge and today, with the easy-to-use and affordable tools that are readily available to anyone with an Internet connection, just about anyone can create one.

For the right person, podcasting can be a great way to expand reach, build brand, increase top-of-mind awareness and create a reputation as a true expert and professional in a given real estate market. But, like any technology or tool, it all comes down to whether podcasting is right for YOU. Start with an honest assessment of whether you have the right skill set, passion and motivation. If you do, start small and give it a try!

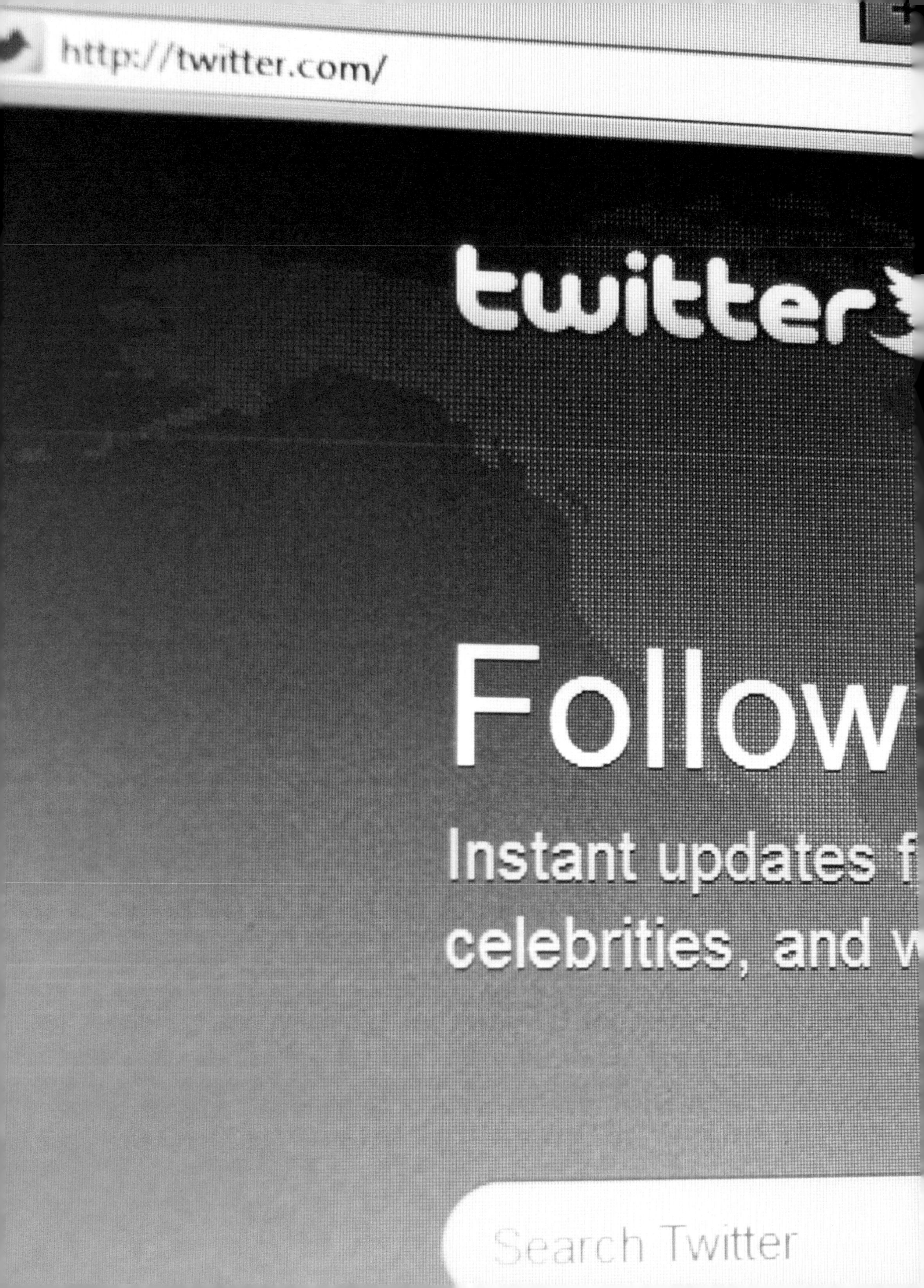

twitter

Follow

Instant updates f

celebrities, and v

Search Twitter

How Tweets Can Make Realtors® More Money

Twitter: The World's Greatest Relationship Creation Machine

How Tweets Can Make Realtors® More Money

Twitter is an online social network that allows users to communicate using text-based messages of up to 140 characters, known as "tweets." The essence of Twitter is sharing information with the people who follow you and receiving information from the people you've decided to follow.

Twitter launched in 2006 and has exploded into a global phenomenon, with over 500 million active users at the end of 2012. It currently generates over 340 million tweets and receives over 1.6 billion search queries every day. It's one of the 10 most visited websites on the Internet. Unregistered users have visibility to the tweets others have written, while registered users can post tweets through Twitter and Twitter clients like HootSuite (hootsuite. com), TweetDeck (tweetdeck.com) and a whole host of apps which have been created for Twitter for mobile devices.

THE SIGNIFICANCE OF TWITTER

For the right real estate professional Twitter can be a great place to initiate, foster and then convert relationships into potential closed transactions. It's often said that Twitter is like the "chamber of commerce meeting that never stops." It can be a great place to connect with new clients, stay connected to past clients and create an amazing array of potential business opportunities. Here are a few facts:

- **Growth:** It took over three years for Twitter to reach its first billion tweets. Now there are

Twitter has exploded into a global phenomenon, with over 500 million active users generating over 340 million tweets and over 1.6 billion search queries every day.

A large study of all major social platforms was done by Pingdom (pingdom.com) and published in June 2012. The report revealed that Twitter users are "middle of the pack" in terms of age demographics (the vast majority being of home-buying age) and lean slightly toward a female audience (see graphics on Page 44 and Page 48, resepectively).

approximately a billion tweets written every three days.

- **Users:** With approximately 500 million users, as a social platform Twitter is second in users only to Facebook, and is currently the fastest growing social platform.

- **More Active:** Twitter users are the most active of all Social Media users, and they share the most

content (see graphics bit.ly/W3fIct).

This first graphic illustrates that Twitter users are—by a large margin—the most likely to share content when compared with users of Facebook, LinkedIn and Google+. This is important because "creating content" is a large part of the behavior that creates relationships, helps you build top-of-mind awareness and leads to the establishment of brand equity on Twitter. If your goal is to expand your reach and connect with new people, this clearly shows that it's a great place for you to create and share content.

The second graphic illustrates the various "activity" levels of the same four Social Media channels. Here we see that Facebook users are seven times more active than Google+ users, while Twitter users are 33 times more active than Google+ users.

LARGER-SCALE SHIFT TO SOCIAL

Beyond the Twitter-specific reasons just noted, there are larger-scale societal and cultural trends at play, which serve to potentially make Twitter even more significant. As an example, the *Harvard Business Review* (HBR) published an article in August 2012 entitled *Marketing is Dead* (bit.ly/ZmAGC7).

Here are excerpts from that article: "Traditional marketing—including advertising, public relations, branding and corporate communications—is dead. Many people in traditional marketing roles and organizations may not realize they're operating within a dead paradigm. But they are. The evidence is clear. First, buyers are no longer paying much attention. Several studies have confirmed that in the "buyer's decision journey," traditional marketing communications just aren't relevant. Buyers are checking out product and service information in their own way, often through the Internet, and often from sources outside the firm such as word-of-mouth or customer reviews."

Amplifying and supporting the points made in the HBR article, the preponderance of the evidence clearly shows that people trust peer recommendations far more than traditional marketing. According to Socialnomics (socialnomics.net), 90 percent of people trust peer recommendations while only 14 percent trust traditional advertising.

This ties back to Twitter because it's one of the primary places where people have "peer–to-peer" interactions on a large-scale, consistent basis. It's where they obtain recommendations from their friends and it's becoming a premier alternative to traditional marketing.

TOP 250 IN REAL ESTATE

Using a variety of resources, we subjectively created our "Top 250 Real Estate People to Follow on Twitter" using follower count. To be clear, we are not suggesting that "follower count" is the goal of Twitter—it isn't. However, we generally believe that, more often than not, there is at least some correlation between follower count and the Twitter user's understanding of how to effectively leverage Twitter

Twitter Top 250 In Real Estate

@Swedal	173,133
@HousingReporter	165,146
@JasonLucchesi	157,463
@McLaughlinChris	149,794
@MadisonMalibu	148,071
@KevinCottrell	95,791
@RobertoMazzoni	92,563
@Zillow	90,345
@LawrenceBland	88,112
@MStreetRealty	79,436
@RealtorRyan	77,463
@SoChristine	84,164
@REALTORS	65,716
@KellyMitchell	65,588
@SomethinRanDumb	65,530
@SkiHomesOnline	59,106
@ProfessionalOne	55,555
@InmanNews	51,551
@ScottDJensen	51,171
@2MRealty	48,422
@YourPowerhouse	47,861
@Century21	46,789
@erealestate_	45,975
@WalidMRealtor	41,901
@GregFleischaker	39,995
@SpencerRascoff	38,756
@ColdwellBanker	38,218
@Shirley_Wise	36,677
@Trulia	36,626
@MIRealEstate	35,007
@TimStephens_	33,146
@REMAX	30,406
@RickKetterling	30,973
@Agentopolis	30,298
@AgentMarkKelly	27,378

Age Distribution On Social Networks And Online Communities

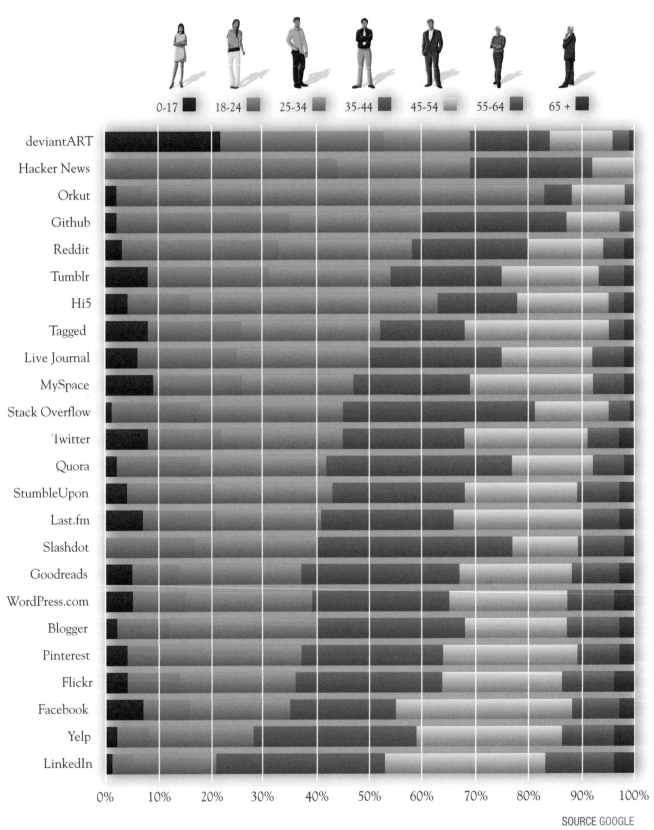

	0-17	18-24	25-34	35-44	45-54	55-64	65 +

deviantART
Hacker News
Orkut
Github
Reddit
Tumblr
Hi5
Tagged
Live Journal
MySpace
Stack Overflow
Twitter
Quora
StumbleUpon
Last.fm
Slashdot
Goodreads
WordPress.com
Blogger
Pinterest
Flickr
Facebook
Yelp
LinkedIn

0% 10% 20% 30% 40% 50% 60% 70% 80% 90% 100%

SOURCE GOOGLE

to build an audience. We suggest you follow all of these people and begin to engage with them. (We apologize in advance for anyone who we have not included but that should have been included due to their follower count.)

SUCCESS WITH TWITTER
Name and Avatar

As a general rule, the best approach is to "humanize yourself." Use your name—or some close derivative—and your photo as your Twitter name and avatar, respectively. Good examples include: @KatieLance, @SherryChris, @NobuHata and @DarinPersinger. There are of course exceptions that have used corporate/brand names successfully by using created-specifically-for-Twitter names. We don't, however, recommend that, as it's fairly time consuming to build a new brand for use on a single Social Media platform.

In this area, a mistake we often see is people incorporating their company name as part of their Twitter handle, for example, "@KWLisa" or "@C21AgentBrown." A change to another company can reduce years of brand building to zero overnight. Regarding your avatar, always use a high-resolution photo that is properly sized to fit the correct dimensions when viewed within Twitter. Low-res photos or photos with the wrong dimensions can actually affect how you are perceived on Twitter, because people see your avatar with every tweet you create.

Case Study

There are many different case studies that demonstrate how to effectively

leverage Twitter in real estate. One example is a blog post that was published on TechSavvyAgent (bit. ly/Z3uord).

This post describes how the author went from having poor results on Twitter (focusing on driving traffic from Twitter to a website) to having a lot of success on Twitter (focusing on "being intentional" and engaging with people) in a very short period of time. The primary takeaways are:

- Don't automate your tweets. Automate in this context refers to scheduling your tweets in advance, so they are sent at pre-determined times when you may or may not be in position to respond should someone seek to engage you.

- Facebook and Twitter are not the same platform, nor do they have the same audience. Twitter is like a cocktail party where there is more of business-focused banter, while Facebook is like a back yard Bar-B-Q, where it's harder to talk shop with family and friends.

- Your behavior online should be the same as your behavior offline.

- It's almost impossible to fully leverage Twitter with the limited functionality of Twitter.com, so use a third-party Twitter client like HootSuite or TweetDeck.

- You must use "columns" to effectively manage Twitter once you reach a certain

@GregCooper	27,370
@KWRI	25,642
@DannyinTampa	25,515
@AlamQ	24,257
@UrbaneMedia	24,078
@92603RealEstate	23,957
@World_Realty	23,905
@CoolShax	23,647
@MayaREGuru	28,060
@WhitneyPannell	23,247
@LouHomePros	22,938
@BenKinney	22,514
@TomFerry	22,374
@OliverGraf360	22,460
@WendyAPatton	22,446
@Swanepoel	22,130
@Auction_Action	21,869
@eRealEstateNet	21,574
@BeachRealEstate	21,271
@rcl4rk	20,968
@HeresyEmail	20,474
@BradHanks	19,935
@1MWilson	19,847
@RETrends	19,505
@CalgaryRealtor	19,488
@Nik_Nik	19,431
@RealtorDotCom	19,168
@DaveWoodson	18,943
@MaikolAkintonde	18,631
@LexHomePros	18,613
@HomeQuestCanada	18,583
@JeffCoga	18,486
@RETrends	18,283
@NaomiTrower	17,663
@RealtyBizBews	17,634
@JeremyBlanton	17,469

volume of activity or otherwise it will overwhelm you. The two kinds of columns you should be using are: (1) people you want to interact with the most (your "VIP" crowd), and (2) the keyword phrases that are most relevant to your business.

- Twitter moves fast and, unlike Facebook where things thread really well and conversations can be carried on for days, weeks and months, Twitter doesn't thread well. So, you need to be "in the moment" if you want to truly leverage it effectively.

- What you're doing by being active on Twitter is staying top-of-mind, seeing what your friends are up to and interacting with the people that matter to you the most.

- There is no secret formula in terms of the number of tweets to send every day or the amount of time to spend tweeting, but once you get beyond the initial hump/learning curve you'll never think of Twitter as a constraint on your time again. Do you think of the time you spend in real life with your friends as a constraint? Then don't think of Twitter that way.

- The most important step of all is to be intentional. That is, focus on Twitter as an engagement tool to keep in touch and communicate daily with the people that matter the most to your business.

The author's results were astounding. Although he didn't focus on inbound links, they went from 30 per month to 600 per month very quickly. The increase in traffic also generated legitimate new business opportunities so the results were very tangible. As we progress through the remainder of this chapter we'll be addressing a number of the key techniques, mindsets and strategies alluded to in this case study.

Best Practices

Here are some practical takeaways and

@MarioRamirez408	17,441
@411Realty	17,422
@NYC_Real_Estate	17,380
@JonathanKarlen	17,329
@GeorgeONeill	20,321
@Chris_Smth	16,554
@VHenry	16,511
@JasonCrouch	16,465
@PhxREguy	14,962
@KWCareers	14,933
@MarkBrian	14,607
@MassRealty	14,550
@Nelsonian	14,388
@JayPapasan	14,143
@VBFalcon	13,840
@TitleExaminer4U	13,830
@JenniferBunker	13,542
@MikeMueller	13,020
@ReggieRPR	12,972
@Corcoran_Group	12,779
@JeffTurner	12,685
@TCar	12,500
@GoHomeMARKeet	12,437
@AndyKaufman	12,058
@sellfast	12,032
@SherryChris	12,030
@MiamiCondoShp	11,968
@AgentGenius	11,845
@UtahREpro	11,758
@Spectrum_Ent	11,725
@RebekahRadice	11,609
@Ines	11,541
@TopRealtorGirl	11,526
@Biznaz	11,443
@REMAXTEAM	10,971
@InsideSeaCoast	10,779

For 100m Users, The Average Number Likely to Share a Story

1ST — 197.3

2ND — 41.8

3RD — 15.2

4TH — 6.0

SOURCE UMPF

philosophies to help you use Twitter successfully:

1. **Relationship:** You need to focus on the relationship, not the transaction. Twitter users have become hypersensitive to "those who sell" and are quick to un-follow those who breach this important Twitter etiquette.

2. **IRL:** Think about whom it is that you would want to interact with "in real life" and then focus on connecting with them on Twitter. It's easy to engage with people from literally all over the world on an infinite array of topics, including some of the most prominent people in real estate.

3. **No Tweet Left Behind:** This means that you should always do your best to reply to every tweet sent to you. People on Twitter can be very fickle, and a way to inhibit the growth of your relationships is to become known as someone who doesn't consistently reply to outreaches from others.

4. **Pay It Forward:** Some of the most powerful relationships created using Twitter can take a long time to develop, and they often involve lots of attempted interactions that don't seem to work. It's important to remember not to have any expectation of a payback.

5. **A Marathon:** To succeed at Twitter, it's important to remember that you're running a marathon, not a sprint. If you're looking for a "get rich quick" scheme, Twitter isn't your solution. Leveraging Twitter is a lot like leveraging a membership at a country club. You can develop some amazing relationships that can turn into big business, but rarely do those relationships develop quickly.

6. **Anywhere, Anytime:** While relationships do often take time to develop, what makes Twitter so exciting is the fact that you can develop them without ever leaving your computer or mobile device. Unlike a country club, which typically requires large membership dues and the need to be in a specific physical location to leverage that networking opportunity, Twitter allows the creation of relationships from anywhere at any time (and it's free).

7. **Forever:** Never tweet anything that you wouldn't want your spouse, your mother or your employer to read. Picture every tweet you write plastered on an enormous billboard on the busiest section of the most highly trafficked highway in your market, and let that be your editorial guide.

8. **Help Others:** In the words of noted pop culture icon and New York Times bestseller Seth Godin: "If you want to achieve your own objectives, help other people achieve their objectives."

9. **Stay Consistent:** Consistency is the key. Keep at it over the long haul, providing quality content and engagement and watch your audience and your influence grow

@MiamiEstates	10,757
@MicahelCasnji	10,592
@BethHeilman	10,477
@DLambrechts	10,460
@cleanslate4u	10,426
@CyndeeHaydon	10,424
@DJMorisInc	10,295
@eMediaRealty	10,249
@Hermanity	9,972
@NYCREMilton	9,904
@Debbie_L	9,726
@LegalLink1	9,606
@DRothamel	9,522
@tdgmoves	9,451
@RealEstateDenvr	9,431
@NaplesProperty	9,381
@TimTerpeningFL	9,253
@LStephenCleary	9,248
@Ribeezie	9,224
@LawyersRealEst	8,849
@TomRoyce	8,843
@TimothyAlex	8,762
@EricJCox	8,655
@Lance_Whipple	8,588
@AmyChorew	8,513
@AndreaRealtor	8,361
@RealtyOptimist	8,253
@KenBrand	8,226
@StaceyHarmon	8,223
@LaniAR	8,153
@KrisstinaWise	8,139
@1000WattMarc	8,101
@RealtorKeita	8,031
@KatieLance	8,027
@SellWithPhil	7,955
@KelleyKoehler	7,575

Gender Distribution On Social
Networks And Online Communities

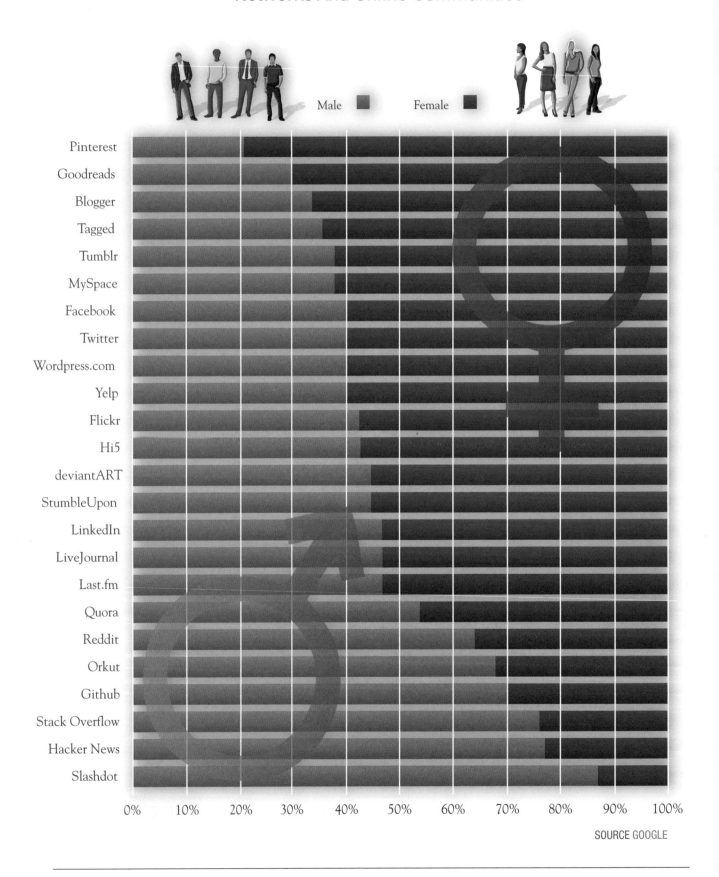

over time.

10. Leverage HootSuite or TweetDeck: You can create columns inside either of these tools that include keywords, specific people on Twitter or just about anything else you can think of. Using these columns is one more way for you to monitor what's going on, and this can be a great way to facilitate more effective and efficient engagement and to identify new information you can share with your audience.

OVERALL STRATEGY

As it's very easy to get pulled off in the wrong direction because the Twitter universe is so diverse, you must have specific objectives tied to a specific strategy or you'll have no idea whether you're accomplishing them or not. As is true for any serious business plan, it's our strong recommendation that you have a formally written and documented Twitter strategy. Once you've identified your specific strategic objectives you can then focus on building specific campaigns to accomplish them. Some objectives you may wish to consider are lead generation, being perceived as a local expert and client retention.

1. Lead Generation

Twitter can be an effective lead generation tool. However, you need to understand a few things up front:

- Twitter is not a traditional "lead generation" tool like an IDX search on a website. IDX connections can be nearly instantaneous, when

a person signs up to search for homes on your website you're notified immediately, which can position you to immediately reach out to that person almost in real time, right as they're thinking about real estate. Twitter isn't like that because the odds of someone thinking about real estate at any given point in time are obviously fairly low.

- As compared to most traditional lead generation methods, Twitter is typically a slower, more methodical process. Again, think "online country club." If you keep Twitter in this context, in which the focus is the building of multiple quality relationships over an extended period of time, it can be a very effective tool for developing clients.

- Avoid selling at all costs. As already noted, overt, direct selling is a major turnoff on Twitter.

- Create peripheral content and share it with your followers. You want people to understand that you're in real estate, but you don't want to push them away by being overly aggressive with your sales approach.

Those things being said, what are the most effective things to tweet about if the goal is lead generation? Here are some specific techniques agents have reported as being effective in creating connections that lead to the

relationships that can lead to sales:

- Blog about the geographic location where you sell and tweet about that.

- Take lots of local pictures

@TeriConrad	7,552
@RhondaDuffy	7,486
@SusanGoulding	7,478
@ChrisJSewell	7,440
@LorenSan	7,409
@JanieC	7,365
@JasonJakus	7,326
@AZRealProperty	7,312
@ChristopheChoo	7,226
@JimDuncan	7,153
@TBoard	7,106
@BradAndersohn	7,042
@JimMarks	7,028
@RealEstateChick	7,007
@KrisTalk	6,991
@troycorman	6,817
@TruliaPro	6,911
@HarrimanRE	6,767
@KarensReal	6,761
@SueAdler	6,757
@TroyCorman	6,726
@RandySelzer	6,725
@DebBernat	6,718
@TopBrokerOC	6,712
@DebBernat	6,683
@DOverbey	6,596
@LocoHeather	6,647
@DaleChumbley	6,594
@JBurslem	6,528
@AlfredoGuzmanLB	6,481
@Halstead	6,467
@ChadHyams	6,451
@MichelleAmen	6,423
@DeanOulette	6,422
@BillLublin	6,384
@LHuntington	6,302

and include them in tweets.

- Shoot walking tours of local places of interest, post them on Vimeo (vimeo.com) and/ or YouTube and embed links in tweets.

@LisaArcher	6,224
@LauraMonroe	6,189
@KR_Tweets	6,167
@JRDorkin	6,134
@TO_realestate	6,128
@LesleyLambert	6,076
@FlashPreviews	6,027
@RealLifeSheri	5,987
@RayProsek	5,936
@EricStegemann	5,903
@MikeSomonsen	5,865
@RichardSilver	5,809
@ToddWaller	5,807
@NickRatliff	5,780
@_CT_RealEstate	5,768
@MiamiBeach	5,764
@OhioAgent	5,725
@CameronTeam	5,692
@MoKnowsHomes	5,641
@LolaMcIntyre	5,609
@SydHarew	5,585
@BrandWendy	5,583
@RobHahn	5,523
@IslandAgent	5,478
@FloridaSunSales	5,409
@DianeGuercio	5,328
@BRoss	5,325
@DebbieBremner	5,276
@MDSuburbs	5,162
@REWebCoach	5,130
@MichelleRealtor	5,128
@SothebysRealty	5,126
@SBonert	5,121
@MattDollinger	5,099
@AkronOhioHomes	5,084
@MaureenFrancis	5,084

- Interview local people (VIPs, business owners, etc.) and create blogs or videos about them and Tweet about that content.

- Host and promote Tweetups for local residents, inviting people who are house hunting or thinking about selling.

- Encourage as many people as possible in your community to join Twitter and add them into one or more Twitter lists. Then make a point of engaging those people as often as possible on topics that matter to them.

- Explain the home buying process with a series of videos and tweet links to the videos.

- Tweet about other local things of interest.

From a lead generation perspective a key thing to note is that you are using Twitter as part of a larger Social Media strategy, which would typically include things like a blog, a Facebook business page, a YouTube and/or a Vimeo channel, etc., in which you are using Twitter to drive people to those places where you've created that "peripheral to real estate" content. Twitter becomes very valuable in this sense because of your ability to leverage the platform to reach a lot of people. It's often the optimal delivery system for the content that you create in other places.

2. Become the Local Expert
Twitter can be an excellent tool to build brand awareness and to position

you as "the local expert." Here are some things you can do along these lines:

- Make videos of your clients giving testimonials about you, post them on YouTube and/or Vimeo and send out tweets with links to those videos.

- Take photos of clients standing in front of homes you just sold them and include those photos in tweets.

- Tweet links to places where clients have written positive reviews about you.

- Conduct local seminars about real estate (e.g. "understanding the home buying process," "getting your house ready for sale," etc.) and tweet links to those events.

- Tweet links to your speaking engagements.

- Tweet about any blog posts that you've written of a "client education" nature.

- Write blog posts and/or make videos in response to repetitive questions that you deal with frequently and tweet links to those posts.

3. Client Retention
It's been said that in the long run, a past client is more valuable than a perspective or future client. We happen to agree with that perspective and that philosophy. It's also been said that real estate professionals

How Much More Active Each Channel is Compared to Google Plus

2.5x

7x

33x

Total % Shares

We've also broken these stats down into different news sectors to show how each social media platform is performing. Business stories have the highest percentage of G+ shares, but even this is well behind the other platforms:

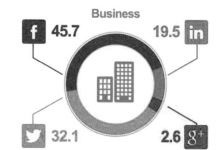

Business

f 45.7   19.5 in

32.1   2.6 g+

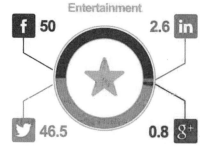

Entertainment

f 50   2.6 in

46.5   0.8 g+

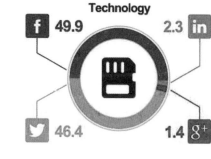

Technology

f 49.9   2.3 in

46.4   1.4 g+

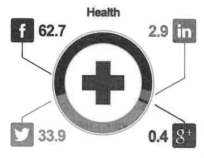

Health

f 62.7   2.9 in

33.9   0.4 g+

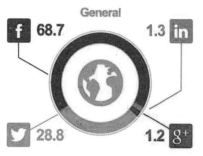

General

f 68.7   1.3 in

28.8   1.2 g+

SOURCE UMPF

@MissyCaulk	5,060
@GlennKelman	4,826
@hklong	4,813
@BHGRealEstate	4,811
@BNix	4,757
@TobyBoyce	4,752
@EPHomes	4,724
@LivingBeaverton	4,715
@SarahElles	4,711
@OzarksAgent	4,709
@PensacolaFLJack	4,694
@MonikaMcG	4,639
@RobDenny	4,629
@RealtorJosh	4,619
@RajQsar	4,528
@OutdoorLori	4,494
@AudieChambrln	4,365
@DarinPersinger	4,359
@Liz_Landry	4,325
@JustinHavre	4,291
@HudsonHomeTeam	4,289
@BlockRealEstate	4,261
@Debra11	4,257
@KingofSurprise	4,240
@Mary_R_Roberts	4,229
@Gahlord	4,169
@ACummings	4,136
@NashvilleBrian	4,121
@SherlockofHomes	4,075
@RealtorTed	4,039
@RealtorJimLee	4,062
@AlbieVas	3,915
@DotLoop	3,875
@VictoriaAgent	3,830
@AskforLara	3,801
@Dakno	3,774

often have a weakness—"not doing a great job of hanging on to or staying in contact with their past clients." Used properly, Twitter can be an excellent way to mitigate that particular problem. Here's how:

- **Locate Your Past Clients on Twitter** - You can do this in a variety of ways, including a personally addressed e-mail blast, a letter, postcard or,

probably the most effective way, a simple phone call. And this has the obvious added benefit of giving you a reason to reach out to every one of your past clients. This

Glossary of Key Twitter Terms

Because of the 140-character limitation of a tweet, Twitter has effectively created a language of its own. Here is a list of the more commonly used terminology and abbreviations in the "Twitterverse" (the social system that is Twitter).

@Reply (spoken as "at reply"): The @ reply refers to a Twitter update (a tweet) that is directed/addressed to a specific Twitter user (note that the terms "tweet," "Twitter post" and "Twitter update" are synonymous). You use @replies when you want to direct something to an individual, as opposed to your entire Twitter following (all the people following you on Twitter, which is what happens otherwise).

DM: This stands for "Direct Message," which is a private message visible only to the sender and recipient of the DM. Note that DMs can only be sent to someone who is following you.

Favorite or Fav: Twitter users can "favorite" tweets, which marks those them for later review by that user. In the world of Twitter, favoriting a tweet is comparable to bookmarking a webpage on the Internet.

Follow/Following/Follower: The term "Follower" is used to describe someone who subscribes to another person's tweets.

#FF: Follow Friday is a tradition on Twitter in which users recommend people they believe others should follow. People have come to summarize this by simply tweeting something like "#FF @JoeSmith @LisaCarruthers," which informs that user's followers that the user thinks they should consider adding @JoeSmith and @LisaCarruthers to the list of the people they follow.

Hashtag: A hashtag, denoted by the use of the "#" symbol, is a way of "tagging" tweets for Twitter's search engines, and also to let other users understand the larger context surrounding a tweet. An example would be "#SUPERBOWL," where a user wants others to understand they are tweeting about the Super Bowl. Further, when you click on a hashtag inside a tweet, you see a stream of all of the tweets written by anyone that has used that same hashtag.

Lists: This is a feature on Twitter that allows a user to create a group of other Twitter users that all have something in common. Lists can be created with two levels of privacy: visible only to the creator of the list or visible to the public. People create lists for a variety of reasons, including prioritizing the tweets of a certain group of people (local VIPs, past clients or real estate influencers, etc.), to share those lists with other people on Twitter, etc.

RT: A Retweet describes a situation in which a user takes a tweet written by some other user and "re-shares" it with their own following, inherently giving the original tweeter full attribution in the process. Within Twitter and every Twitter client (like HootSuite or TweetDeck; see below), there is a basic menu option that allows a tweet to be retweeted with a single click. Some but not all Twitter clients allow the original tweet to be edited by the user before retweeting the original tweet. tweets are generally retweeted because a user likes something about the original tweet and simply wants to share it with their Twitter followers.

is just a matter of asking people what their Twitter name/handle is. Another way to do this, although probably a lot more time consuming and cumbersome (because people so often use Twitter handles that are not logical or obvious), is to do Twitter searches using your clients' names.

- **Create a Past Client List on Twitter** - You can create lists on Twitter and populate them with specific individuals you're following. You can then observe the things that those in a given group are tweeting in a single, convenient place (Google "create list on Twitter"). Create a Twitter list that includes all of your past clients, and place that list where you can easily observe it when you're using Twitter. An example would be a column on HootSuite or TweetDeck or a list on any other Twitter client or Twitter.com.

- **Engage and Counterpunch -** Continuing the prior point, as you are observing the Twitter behavior of your clients in your past client list, simply "counterpunch" based upon what you see them Tweeting about. What we mean by that is to just react naturally and organically to whatever your past clients are tweeting. If a past client tweets about their son's soccer game, simply offer your congratulations on a win or an encouraging word in the aftermath of a defeat,

Trending Topics: Trending topics are popular topics that are being tweeted about at the highest relative level within Twitter at any particular moment in time. This simply means that more tweets are being written using a specific hashtag than other tweets that are being written using other specific hash tags. Examples of common trending topics are major sporting events, major news events, opening days of movies, etc. Users can discover trending topics a variety of ways depending upon whether the user is using Twitter or some other third party Twitter client. Monitoring trending topics is a great way to stay current with regard to major breaking stories and events.

Tweeps: The people that use Twitter. Not commonly used when referring to your Twitter friends.

Tweet Stream (or "Timeline" or "Twitter feed"): When you choose to follow another person on Twitter that user's tweets appear in reverse chronological order in your "timeline" or "Twitter feed."

If you follow 20 people, for example, you'll see a mix of tweets (in real-time or near real-time) scrolling down the page (if you are using Twitter.com, or in a column if you're using a Twitter client) in what is known as a "Tweet stream." You can also view the tweets written by people you're not following by simply searching for them inside Twitter and reading their Twitter page. But the more common approach is to follow people of interest and discover their tweets as part of your tweet stream.

Twitter Client: This refers to a third-party application designed to better manage and organize your Twitter experience. The two most popular are HootSuite and TweetDeck. Both allow users to organize and view Twitter in ways that are generally perceived as superior to what you will experience if you simply use Twitter. They include a whole range of features, options and functionalities not found on Twitter. Most people start using Twitter and then transition into one of these third-party clients when they

realize Twitter's limitations. Similarly, there is a wide range of Twitter apps that have been built for Smartphones and tablets. It's estimated that fewer than half of all tweets are written using Twitter, based on an analysis of 500 million tweets by Sysmosos (sysmos. com).

Un-follow or De-Friend: This describes the situation when someone un-subscribes from receiving another user's tweets. This can happen for a variety of reasons, all of which can be summarized by saying that the un-friending user simply wasn't receiving sufficient value or was somehow offended by the tweets of the un-friended user.

URL Shorteners: Because tweets are limited to 140 characters it makes sharing long web links (which people very often do) difficult. By using a link-shortening service, users can share long URLs with their Twitter followers. Most Twitter clients do this URL shortening automatically.

etc. Stay front and center in your past clients' minds without being salesy.

CONTENT CURATION

The term "curate" has become popular of late. In its simplest terms, what that means is "locate content you believe will be valuable to your audience and share it with them." Here are some steps you can take to curate content and build a larger, more loyal and more engaged audience:

1. **Google Alerts.** You can use Google Alerts (google.com/alerts) to track keywords you think are relevant to your clientele. Examples might be "name of your town," "name of your town real estate," etc. Google Alerts will then email you directly whenever these keywords appear on the Web. This can provide you with a nearly infinite stream of great information to use in your Tweeting to help keep you engaged with locals on the things that matter the

Glossary of Key Abbreviations

Ab/abt	About
b/c	Because
b4	Before
cld	Could
F2F	Face to Face
FTL	For the Loss; a sarcastic way of saying you don't like something
FTW	For the Win; a sarcastic way of saying you like something
IDK	I Don't Know
IRL	In Real Life
OH	Overheard; I Overheard

From the Vault: Real Estate Confronts Reality (1997)

"Technology will emerge as the single largest contributor to the way real estate agents interact with their customers."

most to them.

2. **Google Reader.** Google Reader (google.com/reader) is a content application and platform provided by Google that is an aggregator of content served by web feeds. Stated differently, it's a tool you can use to organize RSS feeds of the websites or blogs that consistently have content that could be of interest to your clients. This is basically identical to Google Alerts, except in this case you're identifying specific URLs that have content you like, as opposed to keywords, which are what drives Google Alerts.

3. **Filter.** By collecting information using the two prior points you will now have a steady stream of potentially quality content to share with your followers. This is where the "art of curation" comes into play, because not all of that information will be valuable to your audience.

4. **Share.** A key thing to keep in mind is this: only share quality

content. You're better off sharing fewer things of higher quality than more things of lesser quality. Use your judgment and see how people react to what you're sharing. Do more of what produces quality engagement and less of what doesn't.

OTHER STRATEGIES AND CONSIDERATIONS

1. WIIFM

What's in it for me (WIIFM) may sound very self-centered, but experience has taught us that most people operate almost exclusively from that perspective. So to be successful on Twitter you need to do the opposite and serve and help others. Your focus must be on providing information that your target audience will want to consume. This is something that people often don't fully grasp when they enter the world of Twitter, and as a result newcomers frequently don't get the results they expect. They then blame the platform when the real culprit wasn't Twitter, but rather simple human nature.

2. Know Your Audience

Knowing your audience is crucial for success with Twitter. The hard reality is that it's impossible to know your entire audience (unless your

audience is very small in size, which would run counter to the overall philosophy of expanding your reach using Twitter). Having said that, here are some things you can do to better know your audience:

- Read the user profiles that are visible on Twitter. Remember, what people write in their Twitter profiles is what THEY consider most important about themselves. By simply reading those profiles you can learn a lot about what really matters to those you're engaging.

- Search for content that aligns with the likes and preferences of the most important people in your Twitter sphere.

- Serve up content that matches what you know about your audience. Keep doing that consistently, over and over, without focusing on the results.

3. Take it Offline

From a lead generation/ROI/monetizing perspective, "taking it offline" is a critical concept to understand and leverage. This means connecting with people IRL. The first step in the process is to take the relationship far enough to feel comfortable with the subsequent steps. Do that through consistent engagement, knowing your audience and serving up the content your audience wants. Once you've done that, you can move on to transitioning from online to offline (e.g., invite people out for a cup of coffee, or a meal, host a Tweet-up in which you invite a number of local people to a common place at a fixed time to mingle and connect, etc.). At that point you'll find yourself in the traditional F2F world where people transition from "acquaintances" into "clients" much more readily.

THE DO'S AND DON'TS

Tweeting, as with most Social Media platforms, is highly subjective. But, as a general rule, if a tweet doesn't fit into one of the following categories, think before sending it.

The Do's

- **Inspire:** What makes a leader great? They inspire, and the same goes for great Tweeters. Write things that inspire people and you'll have more followers than you'll ever need.

- **Share:** This is the very essence of Twitter—sharing quality content. This is the power of peer-to-peer recommendation and why many consider Social Media the greatest cultural shift since the Industrial Revolution.

- **Educate:** We've learned SO MUCH from other people

on Twitter. Be that person who shares knowledge—that's cool.

- **Entertain:** Everyone loves to be amused. Entertain and the world will follow you.

The Don'ts

Here are some general guidelines of things to avoid while tweeting:

- **The Three C's:** Dale Carnegie said it so well, "Any fool can criticize, condemn or complain, and most fools do." Don't be a critic, a condemner or a complainer, except when truly warranted and then in moderation.

- **Arguing:** Healthy, respectful debate is one of our favorite aspects of Twitter. Having a brawl in public? Not so much.

- **Triviality:** This gets to the heart of the debate over the optimal "signal-to-noise" ratio on Twitter. Over time we find that we tune out the people who share too much trivia.

SUMMARY

Clearly Twitter isn't for everyone. Like any other technology or social platform, it can be a great help or a great distraction to your business. It just depends upon how effectively you use it and whether you leverage it correctly.

If you want to use this platform successfully, be consistent, sincere and authentic, just like IRL. Be interested

in other people and communicate with them honestly, organically and frequently. This is where Twitter can be so powerful and so special because the platform affords you the opportunity to communicate with an almost infinite number of people on a level far more expansive than what you could ever realistically do in your normal, physical environment.

So, if you are technically oriented and enjoy communicating with people on a consistent basis, and if you understand that relationships take time to develop, then you will most likely find Twitter to be a great medium for you. We strongly recommend you give it a try.

4 Why A Video Is Worth 1.8 Million Words

Video: The Next Big Thing In Real Estate

Why A Video Is Worth 1.8 Million Words

Traditional real estate marketing has historically been limited to paper (think newspaper ads, glossy color brochures and floor plans). While these methods can be effective, they are for the most part lifeless and limited by their "two dimensionality." This means that such techniques simply can't effectively show how people live in a home or in the larger community, and there is often little or no context on where this home fits in the neighborhood.

But we all know a home is more than a collection of bedrooms, bathrooms and granite countertops. It's a place where people move in and around rooms, where there are neighbors, solitude or a unique ambience; it's a lifestyle and it's down the street from something awesome. There is that unique, small spot where the sunset is especially stunning, or that specific corner of the yard which is always cool, even in the heat of summer.

These small, potentially important nuances that can make or break the marketing of a home are nearly impossible to convey with photos, but video can transcend what came before it. Video can take a consumer inside a home and show how the rooms flow, allow them to visit the park or the coffee shop and see life as it unfolds before the camera. It helps the consumer feel the pulse of a neighborhood and shows the viewer how life could be, if they lived in this home.

To date, video in real estate has been quite limited, at least in terms of the percentage of the people in the industry who actually use it. For the most part, it's consisted of "video home tours"—often marginally produced by agents themselves, or done by professionals—and little else. However, changes—in terms of consumer demand, affordability of equipment and increased ease of use of editing software, etc.—are ushering in a new era of video in real estate.

It's widely acknowledged that YouTube is the number-two search engine, behind only Google. According to comScore (comscore.com), 84.9 percent of the U.S. Internet audience has viewed online video and the average Internet user in the U.S. watched a staggering 1,150.2 minutes of video in December 2012—that's over 19 hours in one month (see chart on page 59).

VIDEO IN REAL ESTATE

Until recently, video was not that easy to use and/or not cost effective for many real estate professionals. However, recent changes in both technology and equipment now make video a viable marketing tool for almost any agent. Camera equipment, editing software and the ability to host and promote video to a large, relevant audience are all now relatively cheap, easy to use and widely available. For those who lack the time or ability, professional videographers can often produce these videos at a reasonable cost.

Sellers Want It

According to the National Association of REALTORS® *2012 Profile of Homes Buyers and Sellers* survey, over 72 percent of homeowners felt that video was an important part of marketing their home. And yet, only 3 percent of Realtors® used video in their regular marketing. This clearly points to a potentially enormous competitive advantage available to those who will embrace video.

Buyers Use It

According to the same study, "Virtual video tours" ranked as the third most "very useful" website feature for all Internet-using buyers. In the NAR study entitled The *Digital House Hunt*, which details the ways in which buyers use technology in the real estate process (see chart on Page 62), the four biggest reasons that buyers use video were:

- To find out more about a specific community (86 percent).
- To tour the inside of a home (70 percent).
- To obtain general information (54 percent).
- To compare features across multiple companies (44 percent).

TYPES OF VIDEO

The following primary types of video are frequently used in real estate:

1. **Home Tours:** Walk through of homes without physically being there.

2. **Branding:** Reasons why buyers and sellers should want to work with you and/or your team or company.

3. **Lifestyle/Community:** Stories that paint a picture of what it's like to live in a specific city or town in an attempt to connect with clients on a deeper emotional level.

4. **Testimonial:** Past clients talking about what it was like to work with you and/or your team or company.

5. **Educational/Tutorial:** Explanations of processes that teach and inform clients or other agents.

BEST PRACTICES

1. Home Tour Videos

This is, by far, the most frequently created type of video in real estate, and logically so as this is the second-most popular reason Internet buyers want and use video. We suggest that you have quality home tours created for all of your listings where the price point and condition of the home warrant such investment. In many markets, professional videographers offer real-estate specific packages at reasonable prices (e.g. obeo.com, homeviewllc.com, agentcasts.com, etc.).

If you choose to do it yourself, make sure you're using suitable equipment and that your finished product is good enough to present the property in a positive light. Our experience is that most DIY home tours are not done well, although there are certainly exceptions to that rule. Toward that end, we recommend that you get honest feedback from other people to help you objectively evaluate your own work. Something we've heard many times is this: "When it comes to marketing real estate, no photo is better than a bad photo." We think this applies to video probably even more so.

Top US Online Video Content Properties
(Ranked by Unique Video Viewers - Dec 2012)

Property	Total Unique Viewers (000)	Videos (000)	Minutes per Viewer
Total Internet : Total Audience	181,717	38,673,322	1,150.2
Google Sites	152,971	13,181,969	388.3
Facebook.com	58,776	419,959	16.4
VEVO	51,640	592,463	39.3
NDN	49,942	510,319	69.5
Yahoo! Sites	47,516	383,514	51.5
AOL, Inc.	42,425	692,467	55.0
Viacom Digital	42,334	431,833	39.4
Microsoft Sites	40,604	472,812	39.4
Amazon Sites	38,129	138,968	10.3
Grab Media, Inc.	34,911	203,512	28.8

SOURCE COMSCORE VIDEO MATRIX

2. Branding Videos

Video about you, your team and/or your company can be among the most powerful, compelling and effective marketing you can do. Video done well in this area can produce significant ROI and brand awareness. Here are some ideas for branding videos you might create:

- Explain your "USP" (unique selling proposition).

- Personalize yourself by explaining who you are as a human being; your interests, your background, your hobbies, etc.

- Create a "video resume" that briefly describes your professional accomplishments and experience.

- Create a "hybrid video" that includes a mixture of both your video resume and several client testimonials.

- If you DIY your video home tours, "star" in them by doing something that shows your personality.

- Create a video "header" or "trailer" (a few seconds of intro that you include at the start of every video you make) that includes your logo, your image, some appropriate music, etc. and use it consistently.

3. Lifestyle/Community Videos

This is the type of content that buyers want most; as they frequently choose the area they want to live in before they start looking at specific homes. Videos that showcase lifestyle, a neighborhood and/or a town/city are also great uses of your marketing dollar because this kind of content, by definition, has a longer lifespan than home tour videos.

Desirability / Usability of Features on Agent Websites

Features	Very Useful	Somewhat Useful	Not Useful	Did Not Use / Not Available
Photos	84%	14%	1%	1%
Detailed Information about properties for sale	79%	19%	0%	1%
Virtual Video Tours	45%	33%	10%	12%
Real Estate agent contact information	44%	34%	13%	10%
Interactive Maps	41%	34%	11%	15%
Neighborhood Information	34%	44%	12%	9%
Detail information about recently sold properties	33%	41%	15%	11%
Pending Sales / Contract Status	30%	35%	19%	17%
Videos	21%	33%	20%	27%
Information about upcoming open houses	20%	31%	25%	24%
Real Estate news or articles	8%	26%	29%	37%

SOURCE NATIONAL ASSOCIATION OF REALTORS®

From the Vault: Real Estate Confronts Reality (1997)

"With the changes that technology is bringing, real estate practitioners will become more like advisors and facilitators, helping guide consumers, mainly buyers, through the clutter of information and confusion of the home buying process."

We therefore recommend that you create community videos about every neighborhood/community in which you do or want to do business, as well as videos about the key businesses and influential people, places and things in those markets. Because of the "evergreen" nature of these videos, this is a place where you might want to hire a professional to create the most finished and polished product possible. Also remember to tag your videos with all the appropriate keywords.

4. Testimonial Videos

Also per *The Digital House Hunt* survey, other large uses of video are to "compare features across multiple companies" (44 percent), "watch customer testimonials" (30 percent) and "decide which company to purchase from" (25 percent). All of these activities boil down the same basic point: home shoppers are using video to research potential agents or real estate companies.

Video allows people to "meet you before they meet you" and to help them decide whether or not they feel comfortable with you. People ultimately want to work with someone they like, trust and respect, and the way you look, the words you choose, the pace and tone of your voice and the manner in which you dress all communicate volumes about

you as a person and as a professional. If you're going to spend money to have video done professionally, this is another place to do it.

5. Educational Videos

Educational videos are a great "bang for the buck" way to demonstrate your expertise. This is one of the most overlooked categories of video. Home shoppers are looking for knowledge and valuable information in a short period of time. More and more, people are self-educating in every aspect of life. So, if you can be the one to provide that educational content to people looking to buy homes in your market, this can create real opportunity to connect with potential clients. Crisply laid out nuggets of knowledge, snappy graphics and a dedication to "one topic, one video," will go a long way to both educate a potential client and establish an image of authority in the market place. You might consider creating educational videos that explain:

- The specific steps in the home buying and home selling processes.

- Each major section of the real estate contract that you use.

- The difference between "pre-qualification" and "pre-

approval" and the mortgage process in general.

- The best ways to choose a real estate agent and/or a real estate attorney.

- The home inspection process.

- Everything you need to know about buying a condo.

- How homeowner's associations work.

In most cases, in order to create educational videos you will need software that can record everything that happens on your computer screen as well as your voice as you narrate and turn this into a video. Popular choices are Screenflow (telestream.net), Camtasia and Jing (both techsmith.com). If you're camera shy, this might be a great place to begin your journey into video, as these software packages are the easiest to learn and are quite inexpensive (under $100 or in the case of Jing it's free).

GETTING STARTED/THE BASICS
1. Professional Versus DIY

In considering the question of "professional" vs. "DIY," one must assess the potential shelf life of a video. As previously mentioned, certain categories of videos are going to be relevant and valuable for a long time. A neighborhood showcase or self-promotional video can be relevant for years and might truly benefit from a professional touch. On the other hand, a home tour might only be relevant for a few weeks, and, in some cases, maybe just a few days. You'll need to use your judgment when to DIY and when to hire a professional, but, in general we believe that professional quality is the way to go with any content that is going to have a lengthy shelf life, and also for properties above certain price points, where any hint of DIY will likely not be well received.

Remember that each video will to some extent have an impact on the perceived quality of your brand, regardless of whether it's professionally done of self-produced. If your brand

image is high-end, professional and quality, your videos should not scream amateur or hastily made. The good news: a self-produced video does not have to be grainy or low quality. Advances in equipment and editing software make it possible to produce high quality video inexpensively. In addition, Google and YouTube can help you solve nearly every technical challenge and provide invaluable advice and tips (YouTube even offers limited post-production editing fixes after you've uploaded your videos).

2. The Tools

Equipment can be very basic. A flip camera, Sony Playtouch or your iPhone or iPad can shoot great video under the right conditions. Many of these consumer-grade video cameras

are available for less than $200 and are extremely simple to use. However, they tend to have a very physically narrow focus. In other words, they can only shoot a very small part of a room. You will probably need a special wide-angle lens in order to capture home interiors if you decide to use one of these camera options. An excellent source for inexpensive add-ons for these consumer grade cameras is hdhat.com.

The next level up is the popular compact camera. Most of these cameras shoot great video and have decent wide-angle lenses. However, the microphones tend to be weak and, on many of these options, there is no way to connect an external microphone to the camera. If you're going to narrate a home tour or interview anyone, the compact camera is a poor choice. But if you are going to use one of these, we suggest that you get one that has external audio capabilities.

The last stop (before professional grade) is the lower tier of DSLR cameras, such as the Canon T4i or the Sony Alpha 57. You can get different types of lenses and many have the ability to accept an external microphone for sound. The cost for this class of camera is of course higher. At this point it is important to consider the balance of time and resources against the investment of a professional videographer. If you're going to do a lot of video, and you want quality, it probably will be more cost-effective to invest in one of these higher-end cameras (rather than paying a professional over and over).

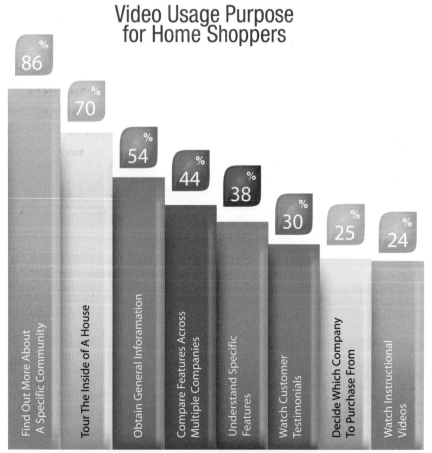

Video Usage Purpose for Home Shoppers

- 86% Find Out More About A Specific Community
- 70% Tour The Inside of A House
- 54% Obtain General Information
- 44% Compare Features Across Multiple Companies
- 38% Understand Specific Features
- 30% Watch Customer Testimonials
- 25% Decide Which Company To Purchase From
- 24% Watch Instructional Videos

SOURCE GOOGLE AND COMPLETE HOME SHOPPER

3. Lighting and Sound

No matter what type of camera you use, sound and lighting play a huge part in a successful video. Of the two, sound is the more important. If anyone is going to talk on camera, consider using an external microphone. They are not expensive and can make a huge difference. Pay attention to background noise. The brain filters out noises like an airplane or a dog barking two houses over, but the microphone picks up everything.

When it comes to lighting, always keep the light source, whether it's the sun, a lamp or a window, at your/the camera's back. Video shot toward a light source almost always looks bad. When shooting inside a home without using special lights, try to film in the morning or late afternoon, when there is less contrast between interior and exterior light levels. When shooting rooms with less natural light you might want to consider using an inexpensive LED light and a reflector.

Professional quality lights are out of the question for most do it yourselfers, but ReelSEO (reelseo.com) has a fantastic tutorial on how to make a light source for under $100 (bit.ly/XLEptG). And a variety of vendors on Amazon offer a wide range of affordable lighting packages that also work well.

Backgrounds are another consideration. When applicable (i.e., when not shooting home tours), an appropriate background complements the message. A purchased backdrop is often a great solution. As many are inexpensive and portable, a backdrop can expand your options and create

> If a PICTURE is worth 1,000 WORDS...
> Then a VIDEO is worth 1.8 MILLION words.
> Dr. James McQuivey

a more professional and consistent look. You might also consider adding a green screen to your video strategy. A green screen allows the video editor to insert any image or video desired into the background during post-production. This is particularly useful for adding a company logo or iconic location served by the agent or brand.

4. Scripting

Not all videos need to be scripted, as some people are very good speaking off the cuff and some topics are better suited for spontaneity. However, for most videos—particularly those of an evergreen nature—scripts are the way to go. Too often an agent will get in front of a camera with only the slightest idea of what they will say. This can result in a confusing message, a lengthy video and a poor image for the creator.

An Emmy award winning film producer and writer remarked, "The problem with real estate videos is that they often do not have a beginning, middle or an end." Storytelling is one of the most effective communication tools known to mankind, and stories must have a beginning, middle and an end. With a little thought and planning this principle can be applied to any category of real estate video.

Organizing your content as a story will help your viewers understand your message, stay engaged while watching the video and apply it to their own situation. A good rule of thumb on scripting is that, for each minute of video, a typical person can speak about 150 words.

Once you've crafted your script, you should practice it a number of times before you actually record anything to perfect the cadence, determine which phrases to emphasize and to get the words pre-loaded in your mind. Various options are now available for creating "virtual Teleprompters" (using an iPad, for example), so you can read your script almost like a TV news anchor would. The more you practice, the better your ultimate quality.

Top 10 Real Estate Individual / Team Channels on Youtube

Name	Subscribers	Views	Youtube URL
1. John McQuiken	3,996	9,864,697	/johnmcquikin
2. Christope Choo	2,201	1,152,326	/christophechoo
3. Jeff Coga	1,231	386,815	/capitalredevelopment
4. Jessica Edwards	1,439	286,406	/thecarolinasfinest
5. Ian Watt	457	210,464	/vancouverpenthouse
6. Cyndee Haydon	870	187,348	/cyndeehaydon
7. Lori Ballen	585	138,700	/richardballen
8. John Coley	58	121,446	/lakemartinvoice
9. Valerie Fitzgerald	421	115,234	/valeriefitzgerald
10. David Pylyp	167	108,270	/dpylyp

3:30 HD

SOURCE CROWDSOURCED BY MICHAEL MCCLURE

5. Editing

It takes a rare talent to shoot a video that is perfect in a single take using only the camera itself. For everyone else, the magic of video is in the editing process. Editing can be as simple as cutting out the verbal miscues, the bloopers and the waste at the start and end of most every video. Editing is where you refine the story, cut out the fluff and get the final product down under the magic one-or-two-minute mark, if possible.

For the more advanced editor, features such as adding titles, transitions, music and still photos can enhance the message and heighten user engagement. Fortunately, both Mac and PC have basic programs for video editing. Relatively simple to learn and use, iMovie (Mac) and Windows Movie Maker (PC) will serve nearly every DIY video maker's needs. However, for those who want to take their video production up another notch, Final Cut Pro X (apple.com/finalcutpro), Sony Vegas (sonycreativesoftware.com) and several other programs offer additional tools and features. These nearly professional level software programs allow for custom transitions, titles and sophisticated effects.

6. Being Seen

It would be a shame to invest all of this time, attention and money if your video was never seen. In fact, the goal is to get as many views of the video as humanly possible.

The best places to do that are YouTube, Vimeo, WellcomeMat (wellcomemat.com) and TubeMogul (tubemogul.com). Beyond that, the key is getting relevant viewers, as a million views from people who are not interested in home ownership has little value. In order to be found by the right people, a video needs an accurate description and appropriate tags that are relevant, one word or short phrase identifiers.

Creating a YouTube Channel is another way to create a relevant audience for the videos. A YouTube channel can serve as a hub for all of your videos. Subscribers are alerted to new uploads and the channel also allows easy social sharing. It can also let the user curate other YouTube videos that have value for the subscribers. The more value you bring to the audience, the more views, engagement and shares you create.

Additional places to promote your video are your website, your blog, via Twitter, via Facebook and on Google Plus. Email is another great way to promote your video and it can be as simple as sending the YouTube link to your database. Also, make sure the video link is prominently featured on all print material as well as the sign rider on the yard sign. Use an easy URL and consider creating a QR (quick response) code to make it easy

Keep Things Short and Sweet
Attention Span by Different Video Lengths

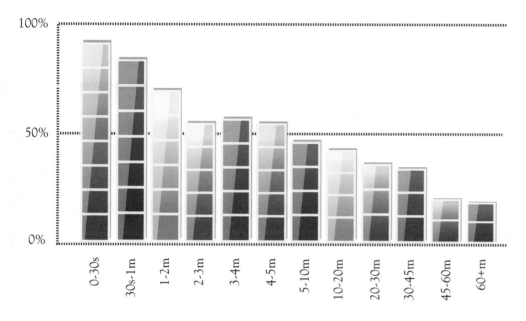

In a study done by Wistia, two videos were shown to their users. The two videos were identical, except that the second video had an extra 10-second clip at the end. On average, the shorter video was watched 72% of the way through, and the longer video was watched 50% of the way through.

SOURCE WISTIA

Put the Goods at the Beginning
Engagement by Video Position

Most videos lose viewership as the video position progress. Interest wanes as viewers get distracted, bored, or realize that the video is not for them. The moral here is: if there's something that you really want people to see, it's best to put it in one the first shots.

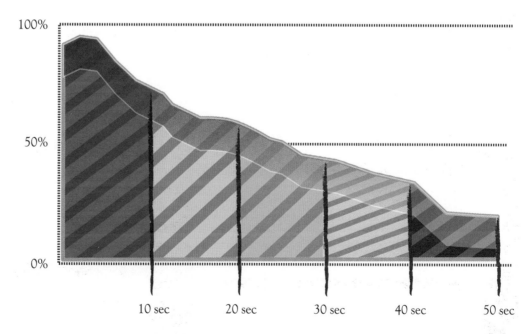

SOURCE WISTIA

Real Estate Video Done Well

CHRISTINE DWIGGINS
Luxury | budurl.com/pezw

Super-luxury video with professional actors and a five-figure budget.

ERIC LAVEY
Luxury | budurl.com/7j5l

Feels like an ad for the HBO series "Entourage."

RICHARD SILVER
Community | budurl.com/s5wa

You feel like you've been to this Toronto suburb after watching this.

CORCORAN GROUP
Branding | budurl.com/97r5

Clever use of canine gets 600,000 views in two months.

ANNE-MARIE WURZEL
Testimonial | budurl.com/s4zt

Great collection of client testimonials with high production value.

HOULIHAN LAWRENCE
Community | budurl.com/vjya

Excellent use of interviews with locals to convey essence of location

KENDYL YOUNG
Video Tour | budurl.com/u5z6

Seller is the star; she completely personalizes and humanizes the home.

GOODLIFE TEAM
Branding | budurl.com/cwjb

Humanizes brand by featuring many of the people in the organization.

KELLEY SKAR
Educational | budurl.com/46lh

Tutorial with over 10,000 views creates goodwill with other agents.

JENNIFER KJELLGREN
Community | budurl.com/bg6n

Nice combination of "about the team" and community expertise.

GREG FISCHER
Branding | budurl.com/f9cx

Does a great job of mixing branding, community and testimonials.

RAJ QSAR
Branding | budurl.com/ep5v

Creator builds his image by promoting a speaking engagement.

IAN WATT
YouTube Channel | budurl.com/ntwv

Model of consistency, with nearly 800 videos, now entering his 6th yr of video.

DANNY DIETL
Lifestyle | budurl.com/v5dk

Excellent "what it feels like to live here" content

SEAN CARPENTER
Branding | budurl.com/fh7q

Heartfelt personal story makes amazing connection with viewers.

to find the video.

Promoting neighborhood, educational and self-promotional videos is a little bit harder, but they are less time-sensitive, so that's not really a problem. A regular habit of posting links to these types of videos in Facebook, Twitter and Google Plus can build a large audience for your video over time. In addition to all of the channels mentioned above, neighborhood videos can be distributed to neighborhood groups and Chambers of Commerce. The online versions of the town newspaper or the local Patch are also possible distributers. Educational and self-promotional videos can also benefit from pay-per-click advertising in the major search engines or in Facebook.

7. Practice and Practice Again

While it is true that it's never been easier to get into video than it is right now, there is still a learning curve and practice makes perfect. Some people struggle with simply being in front of the camera. But take solace in the knowledge that most people are not "naturals," and that many do eventually get comfortable being on camera. If you start and struggle at first, don't be discouraged. If this were super simple everyone would be doing it. If you can get over this initial hurdle, you may find yourself on the other side, having gained a potentially significant competitive advantage in the process.

ADDITIONAL CONSIDERATIONS

1. Start With Power

As the attention span of most viewers is very short (see graphic on Page 65), it's always better to lead with your most important point. This runs counter to what many would think, which is that you would want to save your best information for last. If you do that, your viewer may not be around to see it.

2. Keep it Short

Your goal should be to keep your videos as short as possible. Stick to a single topic and avoid the boring "talking head syndrome" by varying camera angles and adding titles and graphics. Also, when in doubt, if you have the ability to do so, break your video topic down into its "smallest logical increment." That is, record four one-minute videos instead of one four-minute video when possible (see graphic on Page 65).

3. Future Proof It

As technology continues to improve—and as more and more people consume video on "Retina" displays and large HD devices like plasma TVs—the risk of creating content that will one day soon look bad on such devices is real. With that in mind, as you're creating video, you should be thinking in terms of "future proofing" your content.

Matthew Shadbolt is the Director of Interactive Product & Marketing at Corcoran Group (corcoran.com), New York City's largest residential

Top 10 Real Estate Brand/Company Channels On YouTube

Name	Subscribers	Views	Youtube URL
1. Coldwell Banker	5,727	3,747,929	/coldwellbanker
2. Better Homes & Gardens	2,101	2,698,623	/bhg
3. Sotheby's International Reality	3,541	1,807,911	/sothebysrealty
4. Keller Williams	12,616	1,269,811	/kellerwilliams
5. Corcoran Group	1,301	1,155,340	/thecorcorangroup
6. RE/MAX	6,126	909,001	/remaxintl
7. Century 21	2,053	889,588	/century21
8. Partners Trust	334	382,331	/thepartnertrust
9. Frankly Realty	278	170,058	/frannklyrealty
10. Redfin	94	103,605	/redfinvids

3:30 HD

SOURCE CROWDSOURCED BY MICHAEL MCCLURE

brokerage, and was Inman News' Social Media Innovator of the Year in 2011. Corcoran's latest branding video had 600K views in two months, and their YouTube channel has 1.1 million views. Shadbolt said the following:

"So when we're looking at the kinds of technologies that are going to be available to reach new types of audiences—for example, there are very substantial rumors about Apple making a television—if you buy into the idea that that kind of future is coming for all of us, it really starts to impact the quality of what you make right now. So, for example, in terms of real estate video, if you're continuing to film your property tours with a flip cam or hand-held camera in poor lighting and with terrible audio, the idea that that content is going to exist inside of a highly socialized YouTube on an Apple plasma TV, and YouTube moves from being something on the computer to something that's more centered around the home, your content has great risks associated with that kind of future. So this is the kind of stuff that we're looking at right now in terms of the quality and how the quality scales over time. Are you building a product that is going to take advantage of the kind of technology that's coming?"

4. Provide the Benefits

This point is short, but important: to the extent possible, make the focus of your videos about the benefit to the viewer. Tell people how your service is going to make their lives better. As opposed to telling them how wonderful you are and how many homes you've sold. Of course, some

level of "self-selling" is reasonable, appropriate and smart. Just be conscious of the balance between selling "The Benefits" of working with you versus "Your Credentials."

5. Remember to Entertain

Do not underestimate the power of entertainment. Viewers will pay more attention if your video is entertaining or surprising and unusual. A video should not be incongruous with your brand identity, but a little creativity can go a long way toward earning your videos more engagement and attention.

MICRO-VIDEO

A whole new class of applications and tools allows "micro blogging" with video. Ptch (ptch.com), Videolicious (videolicious.com), Vine (vine.com) and Tout (tout.com) are all designed to let users create intentionally-short videos on their Smartphones and tablets and post them to various social networks. The easiest way to think of this new category of video is to compare it to Twitter. At first, Twitter's 140 character limit seemed impossibly short. With 500M users, clearly people have embraced Twitter and gotten past this issue. These micro video applications may fill a similar niche.

Other Notable Real Estate Channels on Youtube

Name	Subscribers	Views	Youtube URL
1. HGTV	11,446	6,148,448	/hgtv
2. Realtor.com	1,445	1,557,696	/realtordotcom
3. Tom Ferry	4,593	922,890	/realestatetrainingtf
4. Zillow	892	726,424	/zillownews
5. HD Hat	415	570,668	/hdhatvideo
6. Productivity Junkies	604	252,888	/besuccessful
7. CDPE	1,562	247,498	/cdpenow
8. Trulia	1,379	208,469	/trulia
9. Inman News	766	147,347	/inmannews
10. Mike Ferry	1,988	187,482	mforganization

3:30 HD

SOURCE CROWDSOURCED BY MICHAEL MCCLU

Agents can use these tools to highlight a feature about a listing, showcase a story in the home buying process or reveal a small slice of community life. Companies can use them to put a human face on the office staff, give sneak peeks of new services or to celebrate milestones. These small videos are probably best used to communicate emotions and to give glimpses of the authentic people behind the scenes. Taken one at a time these videos may not be particularly useful or notable. However, a stream of them, done over time, may help to tell a story that is compelling and authentic. Time will tell if this new trend catches on or falls by the wayside.

WELLCOMEMAT

An alternative to YouTube, or something that can be use in conjunction with it, is WellcomeMat This is a video site specifically developed for real estate that focuses on doing things differently to help create more effective results for real estate professionals. Here are the unique aspects of this site:

- It seeks to drive viewers to view videos on real estate websites, while YouTube seeks to drive viewers to view videos on YouTube; this is a large and important distinction.

- It is optimized for real estate, while YouTube is not.

- It is built to syndicate video out to other video sites, while YouTube is not.

- When you place your videos on YouTube and other sites,

Google naturally biases in favor of YouTube

Christian Sterner, co-founder of WellcomeMat, told us the following: "where the video is viewed matters greatly. When a potential real estate client watches a video on YouTube, they're completely "out of context" from a real estate professional's perspective. When that same potential client watches a video on a real estate website, they're in the perfect context for that agent to benefit from that view. WellcomeMat was designed to help agents maximize the amazing potential of video, and to create what we call "relevant reach" – which in simple terms means getting lots of views from the right viewers in the right places. Obviously, we're biased, but we think the future of real estate is video, and we think all the statistics bear that out. Also, to be clear, we're noy anti-YouTube. In fact, we syndicate to YouTube, if that's what an agent elects. But we think the savvier agents will realize that there is more to be gained from using video as part of their world than as part of YouTube's world."

EXAMPLES OF REAL ESTATE VIDEO

Listed in this chapter are several categories of YouTube channels that we've subjectively identified as examples of real estate brands, companies, teams and agents doing video well. We suggest that you browse some of these channels to see what others are doing that seems to be working, at least in terms of generating views.

SUMMARY

Real estate video is still in its relative infancy. However, those hoping that video is a fad are making a grave mistake. Cisco estimates that 1.2 million minutes of video content will cross the network every second in 2016, and that it would take over six million years to watch the amount of video that will cross global IP networks each month in 2016. Internet video to TV is expected to continue to grow at a rapid pace; increasing six fold by 2016 and traffic will be 12 percent of consumer Internet video traffic by 2016, up from eight percent in 2011. Video-on-demand traffic is expected triple by 2016 and is then expected to be equivalent to four billion DVDs per month.

We should no longer debate whether you should or should not produce video. You just need to decide how. Agents and brokers alike need to pay attention to this tidal wave of a trend. The prevalence of broadband Internet access, combined with the explosive growth of increasingly faster cellular Internet access, has led to consumers watching videos anywhere, anytime, via their mobile devices. Soon, home shoppers will expect to be able to take a video walkthrough on any home they see while standing in front of the house. A home without that video will be at a competitive disadvantage. Potential clients will research agents and companies before setting foot in an open house or a real estate office. An agent with a well-done video will get a meeting. An agent with no video or bad video may never even know that the client existed.

How To Manage Your Digital Footprint

Online Reputation: The Importance of Integrity and Transparency

How To Manage Your Digital Footprint

Remember when E.F. Hutton talked? People listened. People trusted the librarian that the new book by the young unknown author was a good read, and before you knew it the waiting list for the novel was ten people long. If the critic from the local newspaper didn't have a great experience at the new Italian restaurant in town, you could almost hear the editor writing the establishment's obituary. Most people wouldn't spend their hard-earned money on a movie if Gene Siskel and Roger Ebert didn't give it two thumbs up. And if you heard it from Walter Cronkite, it must have been true.

In a pre-Internet world, the few and very often the local shaped our opinions. We made decisions based on information provided by a relatively small, finite number of people that we knew and trusted.

And, of course, we can't overlook the historical power of traditional advertising. For many of us, it's hard to remember—because the power of advertising has been dropping for quite some time—but there was a time when traditional advertising was far more influential than it is today. And then the Internet came along and changed all that.

INFLUENCE POST-INTERNET

In the pre-Internet world, when we needed advice or information about something, we solicited the opinions of the handful of friends or family that we knew and trusted. But that has changed as we now have access to so many more people.

The first thing to acknowledge is that just about everyone

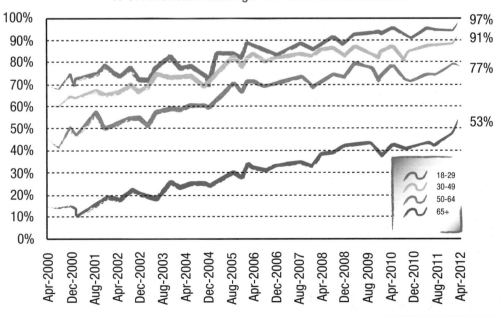

Internet Use By Age Group, 2000 - 2012
% Of American Aduts Age 18+ who use the Internet.

Legend: 18-29, 30-49, 50-64, 65+

Values shown: 97%, 91%, 77%, 53%

SOURCE PEW RESEARCH

is using the web (see chart). Even among the lowest Internet-using demographic (65 old and older) more than half (53 percent) of Americans use the Internet, and at the highest-using strata, fully 97 percent are using the web.

We already know that Social Media platforms have exploded and that the two largest social networks - Facebook and Twitter - each have hundreds of millions of users (see chart on Page 74.). And that creates our new dilemma: "Who do we trust now?"

Because people generally trust peer recommendations but did not previously have easy access to them, the Web has now facilitated an explosion of online review sites that everyone can access.

Pick just about any product and you'll see that most of the meaningful and widely purchased/used products have many reviews. For example, we randomly picked the Canon PowerShot A2300 video camera on Amazon—it has 365 reviews. Go to Yelp (yelp.com) and pick a local bar. We chose the Box Bar in the small community of Plymouth, MI, and it has 53 reviews. Or go to the Apple App Store and select the Camera Plus App—it has 565 reviews. From online retail stores to Angie's List to Google Plus Local (plus.google.com/local), you can hardly surf the web without running into ratings and reviews. They're everywhere.

According to a January 2013 post on Socialomics (socialomics.net):

- 90 percent of consumers trust peer recommendations.

- 14 percent trust advertisements.

- 18 percent of traditional TV campaigns generate a positive ROI.

- 90 percent of those that can TiVo ads do.

- 93 percent of marketers use Social Media for business.

- We will no longer search for products and services; they will find us via Social Media.

- 80 percent of companies use Social Media for recruitment.

So now we have the added power of:
- Reading (and writing) online reviews.

- Asking our extended social networks on Facebook and Twitter for recommendations.

- Googling anything and everything and finding alternatives.

- Using advanced technologies like Apple's Siri to suggest solutions and recommendations for us.

Steve Pacinelli, the co-founder of TechSavvyAgent (techsavvyagent.com) and VP of REALTOR® Events at Move, Inc., shared with us this real life example of how online reputation has impacted him personally:

"My whole family used the same dentist my entire life. I hated that dentist, and for years I had no one credible to ask in terms of finding a new dentist. After yet another uncomfortable experience I decided I'd had enough and looked for another local dentist. I did some simple Google searches and made that decision based entirely on online reviews about local dentists. Fast-forward and today my entire extended family have made the switch to this new dentist; all because of online reviews."

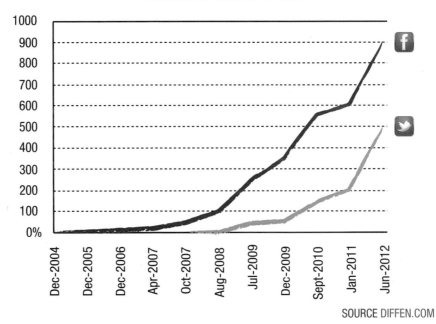

Growth of Facebook and Twitter
Hundreds of Millions of Users

SOURCE DIFFEN.COM

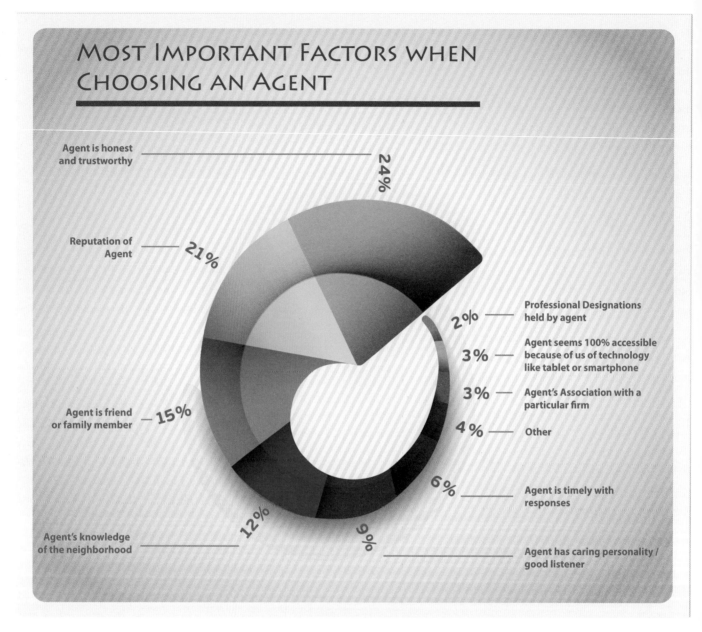

MOST IMPORTANT FACTORS WHEN CHOOSING AN AGENT

Agent is honest and trustworthy — 24%

Reputation of Agent — 21%

Agent is friend or family member — 15%

Agent's knowledge of the neighborhood — 12%

9%

Professional Designations held by agent — 2%

Agent seems 100% accessible because of us of technology like tablet or smartphone — 3%

Agent's Association with a particular firm — 3%

Other — 4%

Agent is timely with responses — 6%

Agent has caring personality / good listener

SOURCE NAR: PROFILE OF HOME BUYERS AND SELLERS 2012

HOW CONSUMERS CHOOSE AGENTS

Each year NAR releases their *Profile of Home Buyers and Sellers* (Profile), which includes a plethora of information about homebuyers, sellers and the real estate professionals who serve them. The Profile seeks to survey consumers who recently experienced a real estate transaction and to better understand their approach to the process and the experiences they had before, during and after their transaction.

Per the 2012 Profile (see chart on Page 77), the "most important factor" people look for when choosing an agent is honesty and trustworthiness (24 percent), and the second is the agent's reputation (21 percent).

The clear point: reputation is very important in real estate. One could argue that fully 45 percent of the decision about which agent to hire is based on reputation, as "honest and trustworthy" certainly go hand in hand with "reputation." Reinforcing this and looking at it from a slightly different perspective, note the following:

- The number one way (40 percent) buyers found their agent was referral by "friend, relative or neighbor." The next method was "Internet Website" (11 percent) and the third was "used agent previously to buy home" (10 percent). All other methods were individually six percent or lower (see table below).

- The number one way (38 percent) sellers found their agent was referral by "friend, relative or neighbor." The next highest method was "used agent previously to buy home" (23 percent). All other methods were individually five percent or lower (see on Page 76-77).

Real Estate Reviews

While online review sites like Amazon, Yelp, Angie's List and Google Plus Local (formerly Google Places) have been around for awhile and have gained a substantial following, most real estate agent review sites are just now starting to find their place in this larger arena. And like much of what happens in the real estate industry, not every one of these sites is created equally. Some things to note as we begin to explore the myriad of real estate review sites:

- You should be aware that you can, and often do, show up on numerous review sites that are indexed on the web, whether intended or not.

- Some sites are "opt in" destinations where you can choose to be reviewed or you might even pay for the opportunity to be reviewed. Others are completely open for any consumer to type in a name and start praising or bashing the services and reputation of any agent. Still other sites require a consumer to build a profile or sign-in so they can be authenticated and verified as real people.

- Most sites where the general public can review an agent don't require any type of verification or proof that the reviewer worked with the agent they're reviewing.

- Knowing how the various sites are monetized is important. Some sites exist simply to attempt to earn referral fees while others attempt to earn income

How Buyer Found Real Estate Agent; First-Time and Repeat Buyers (Percentage Distribution)

	All Buyers	First-Time Buyers	Repeat Buyers
Referred by (or is) a friend, neighbor or relative	40%	49%	34%
Internet website	11%	12%	9%
Used agent previously to buy or sell a home	10%	2%	16%
Saw contact information on For Sale/Open House sign	6%	7%	6%
Visited an open house and met agent	6%	5%	6%
Referred by another real estate agent or broker	5%	5%	6%
Personal contact by agent (telephone, email, etc.)	4%	4%	4%
Referred through employer or relocation company	4%	2%	5%
Walked into or called office and agent was on duty	3%	2%	3%
Search engine	1%	1%	1%
Newspaper, Yellow Pages or home book ad	*%	*%	1%
Direct mail (newsletter, flyer, postcard, etc.)	*%	*%	*%
Advertising specialty (calendar, magnet, etc.)	*%	*%	*%
Mobile or tablet application	*%	*%	*%
Other	10%	10%	10%

* Less than 1 Percent

SOURCE NATIONAL ASSOCIATION OF REALTORS® - PROFILE OF HOME BUYERS AND SELLERS 2012

Method To Find A Real Estate Agent

23% Used agent previously to buy or sell a home.

4% Referred through employer or relocation company.

4% Referred by another real estate broker.

38% Referred by (or is) a friend, neighbor, or relative.

5% Personal contact by agent (telephone, email, etc).

4% Saw contact information on For Sale / Open House sign.

4% Visited an open house and met agent.

from agents. Knowing the motive behind the site can be helpful in terms of judging its ultimate value and objectivity.

- The integrity of information on some of these sites is very much in question (more on that below).

Online Reputation Sites

In the 2010 *Swanepoel TRENDS Report* (Trend #4 – Change By Design) we addressed the issue of consumer ratings: "It is inevitable as the availability of information continues to expand and consumers exhibit the willingness to trust unknown raters on websites on which Realtors® will be rated. It only becomes a question of whether they control their own destiny or allow others to dictate the playing field." Here are a few prominent online sites (in alphabetical order) that you can use to obtain online real estate reviews and/or manage your online reputation:

1. Effective Agents

This site (effectiveagent.org) searches agents "based on impartial research using MLS-based data from the last six months, ensuring that your agent is still in the business and is still performing at the top of his or her game." According to their site, it's a "website owned by a Licensed Real Estate Brokerage Firm, Acuity Real Estate Services, LLC (acuityrealestate.com)."

2. Facebook

Facebook isn't a true agent review site per se, but it remains one of the main places for agents to maintain and build their online reputation. From personal pages to business pages, real estate agents can harness the power of Facebook to build, maintain and develop relationships with people in their local markets, clients they have worked with in the past and other connections around the globe. Agents that find ways to share relevant content in their status updates can earn Likes, comments and shares from their friends. Building unique lists of friends on Facebook is a perfect way for agents to send specific messages to unique audiences as well as keep their finger on the pulse of different communities—geographically and socially. Another outstanding function of Facebook allows agents to build their online reputations through participation in Facebook groups. These specific forums can be either open or private and can create engagement opportunities to share with and learn from fellow agents, as well as to connect with potential clients.

3. Google

As the world's number one search engine and the keeper of everything on the Web, Google is perhaps the

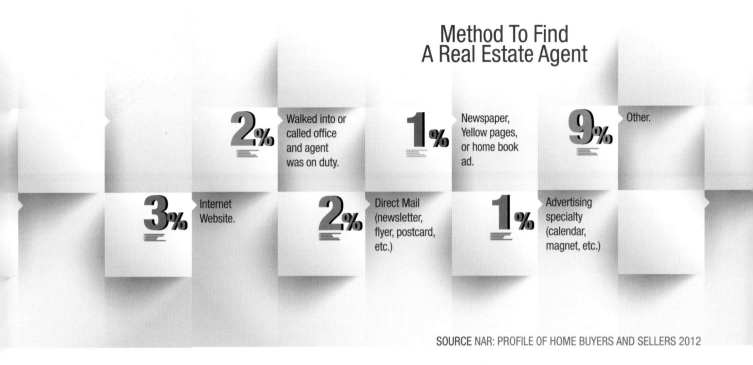

Method To Find A Real Estate Agent

2% Walked into or called office and agent was on duty.

1% Newspaper, Yellow pages, or home book ad.

9% Other.

3% Internet Website.

2% Direct Mail (newsletter, flyer, postcard, etc.)

1% Advertising specialty (calendar, magnet, etc.)

SOURCE NAR: PROFILE OF HOME BUYERS AND SELLERS 2012

ultimate "online reputation" site. It almost always begins at Google for most consumers, especially when they're searching for information related to real estate.

4. Google Plus Local
Google Plus Local helps users discover and share places. The integration of Zagat's (zagat.com) expressive 30-point scoring system gives them detailed insight into businesses before they visit, and Zagat summaries of user reviews helps them decide where they want to go. With Google Plus Local, users can get place recommendations based on their Google Plus circles, their past reviews and their location; publish reviews and photos of their favorite places; read Zagat summaries of user reviews for a place; view the local Google Plus page for a business to see reviews, photos and other useful information; and find reviews from people the user knows and trusts highlighted in their search results.

5. HomeLight
This site (homelight.com) "evaluates agents using transaction data, licensing history, client reviews and Social Media." A key part of this concept rests on ranking agents by their production derived from MLS data.

6. Homethinking
This site (homethinking.com) claims to rank Realtors® by past sales and customer reviews. Per their site, they "measure performance by monitoring real estate transactions to know which houses each real estate agent has sold, for how much and how long on average it took them to do so. There are also user reviews by home owners who have sold their house with the particular agent that helps determine their rank."

7. LinkedIn
One of the "Big Four" social networks, LinkedIn (linkedin.com) is

often considered the "boardroom" of social networking. It's a great place to connect with other business people and to access resumes or business histories. From the perspective of online reputation, LinkedIn is a fantastic place to secure testimonials or "endorsements" of your service and results. The reason this site is so powerful for agent reviews is that each testimonial links back to the reviewer's page. This creates ultimate transparency when the reader can see the page of the person who wrote the review. LinkedIn is also a source of some powerful group interaction and mastermind discussions, as well as potentially creating a network of professionals in other areas that could serve as a powerful referral network among real estate agents across the country and around the world.

8. Mountain of Agents
This site (mountainofagents.com) rates agents using a six category

From the Vault: Real Estate Confronts Reality (1997)

"Digital identities of everyone exist in cyberspace as the Internet links together vast repositories of data…it means that individual privacy is no longer a reality."

approach: knowledge of the local market, transparency with market data, actively involved in the process, trustworthy and compassionate, helpful throughout the transaction and whether the reviewer would feel comfortable referring the agent to friends or family. A real estate agent's rating is comprised of the total number of compliments they've received in each category.

9. RatedAgent

This site (ratedagent.com) claims to have thousands of agent subscribers and to have completed over one million customer surveys, all conducted by a disinterested third-party. The site only sends surveys to consumers who have closed transactions with an agent registered on RatedAgent. Participating agents can display customer service reviews/ratings once a minimum of two surveys have been returned. Three different ratings can be viewed on agent profiles: customer satisfaction rankings, statistics of individual survey questions and seller/buyer comments. Agents "will be asked to agree to and ensure that every completed transaction moving forward be included in the survey process."

10. RealEstateAgent

Promoted as a "win-win" website for

consumers and real estate agents, this site (REA; realestateagent.com) proclaims that they are "very selective" about which agents they will accept as "advertisers" and who they will allow to be promoted or featured. Agents can join the site for as little as $28 for three months or $99 for a full year. This allows REA to assume the difficult task of maintaining an "expensive pay-per-click keyword campaign." The site claims to have no referral fees built into leads that are generated through visitors to the site. Agents who commit to advertising on REA appear to get a landing page that consumers can click on once they find the agent in a search and then pass through to the agent's personal website for inquiries and possible lead generation.

11. RealEstateRatingz

This site (realestateratingz.com) is part of the Ratingz Network, a family of websites dedicated to helping consumers find the best businesses, places, services and products by sharing ratings and reviews. The site "Lets users anonymously rate real estate agents. Users can also post comments and see the public comments posted by others. This site is also a useful scorecard, to find out what consumers are really thinking."

12. Realtor.com

On this site a consumer can search by agent, team or company or can just enter the desired area or the name of the agent. The search method does favor the agents with last names beginning with the letter "A" as it displays Realtors® alphabetically by default. If the agent has "claimed their profile" and added information, the site will show more information about the agent including their average sale price as well as provide a link to the agent's current inventory of homes for sale.

13. SocialBios

This site (socialbios.com) allows individuals and companies to create one social hub for their online profiles through interactive "About Us" pages that simplify the discovery of shared connections on Facebook, LinkedIn, Twitter, Foursquare (foursquare.com) and Google without sacrificing their privacy. The site also can be used to syndicate reviews across various sites and platforms.

14. Trulia

Primarily a site for consumers to search for homes, the site also has the ability for visitors to "Find a Pro" right from the home page. In order for an agent to show up near the top of a local search, it helps if they have been active in the Trulia communities such as Trulia Voices (trulia.com/voices). According to Trulia, "Points are awarded to members based on their contributions to Trulia Voices (Q&A and Blogs) and the recognition those contributions receive; Thumbs Up, Best Answer, Comments and Page Views." Agents can also create or update their profile online and ask anyone to visit their site and recommend them.

15. Twitter
As one of the major social networks available to today's connected consumer, Twitter is not a specific real estate site but it does give people

16. Verified Professional Agent
This concept (verifiedagent.com) seeks to create a "Certified Public Account-like" equivalent for the real estate industry. The site objectively verifies a number of key "critical client service characteristics," including third-party verification of the agent's full time status, experience above the industry norm, a track record of client satisfaction, the respect of fellow real estate agents and a clean record of ethical conduct. The idea is to allow an agent to objectively prove that they are a professional with credentials clearly above the industry norm.

18. YouTube
As the world's second most popular search engine, agents who leverage YouTube can utilize video testimonials or reviews to begin to capture the eyes and ears of consumers. Searching the term "real estate agent" yields 83,400 results while "real estate agent reviews" drops the number to 4,400. Based on those statistics, and given that over 800 million unique users visit the site each month, YouTube still appears to be a location for "early adopters" to the agent review game (see chapter #4 on Video for more details).

> The "most important factor" people look for when choosing an agent is honesty and trustworthiness (24%), and the second most important factor is the agent's reputation (21%).

access to many of the industry elite. Using the search function of the site (twitter.com/search) can help users find any specific conversation or people who have knowledge or input concerning the subject in question. Agents can build a tribe of fellow agents, clients or local consumers or even connect with total strangers though this micro-blogging site. Agents or brokerages can keep connected to their followers and oftentimes enhance their image by having their information shared by others, creating trust through third-parties (see chapter #3 on Twitter for more details).

17. Yelp
Founded in 2004 as a community-sourced review site, Yelp averages more than 80 million unique monthly visitors and claims more than 33 million reviews. Real estate reviews are becoming more popular on Yelp in certain parts of the country, and agents can set up their business profile for free. Creating an account gives the agent a location to direct consumers to so they can leave reviews of the services and expertise provided by the agent. Yelp search will become even more popular in the future as Apple's IOS devices have integrated Yelp reviews into the searches done through Siri voice activated queries.

19. Zillow
On Zillow any agent can create a free profile that provides clients with the ability to leave an agent review. Zillow manually checks every submitted review prior to publication to ensure they meet their Review Guidelines. Agents can secure reviews simply by sending clients a link. Reviewers must create a free profile as no anonymous reviews are allowed. Additionally, the reviewer must have had a working relationship with the agent—agent-to-agent reviews are not allowed. Real estate professionals can also earn Zillow Local Expert and Zillow All Star recognition based on their contributions to the site in

the form of answering questions on Zillow Advice, uploading photos and making other forms of user-generated contributions.

Caveat Emptor

While reviewing the reputation sites above, we encountered a number of things that gave us pause regarding the overall veracity of many of them. Here are a few examples that troubled us:

- On one site, when searching for a Realtor® in Columbus, Ohio—an area that boasts over 5,000 members of the local Columbus Board of REALTORS® — only 2,499 agents were found. Also worth noting was that when doing a search for a community local to us, among the many "top agents" the site suggested was an agent who has been dead

home page, there are over 157,000 agents in the system, and yet there are less than 11,000 reviews.

- It is unclear how one site intends to get the "resume" of an agent, especially since they are in such a small percentage of the real estate markets nationwide as of this writing. We did a few random searches for long-term high-profile agents we know and nothing appeared in a number of these searches.

So while some of these sites do provide great value, do your homework before deciding which sites to leverage to help build your online reputation.

TRANSPARENCY AND INTEGRITY

Beyond the technical/systemic

included these comments in the specific context of online reviews: "People are always going to try to game the system." And "By some estimates, as many as 30 percent of online reviews are complete fakes." While we were discussing this issue on Twitter soon after this news came to light, Tom Royce of Royce Interactive (royceinteractive.com) Tweeted the following with regard to the issue of the fidelity of online review information: "I know a couple guys who have over 50 personas to manage fake reviews for clients."

In another example specific to real estate, Realtor-complaints.com—a website which appears to have been created for the sole purpose of extorting money from real estate agents—was shut down. As reported in RealtyTimes on January 29, 2013: "An investigation by real estate trade

> In today's Internet-driven world you people will Google so you might as well do all you can to maximize the "good" and to minimize the "bad" results.

for over four years.

- With just a little more than 1,500 agents on another site there aren't a lot of agents to choose from, so one could argue "how can you assure me of getting a great agent when less than 1 percent of all agents in the U.S. are on the site?"

- On another site, according to statistics displayed on the

challenges noted above, with so many places where anyone with access to the Internet and an opinion can leave a review—whether they've worked with an agent or not, whether verified or not, whether honestly or wrongly intentioned—the integrity of online review information is being called into question more and more frequently.

As one example, in October 2012 ABC News aired a report that

association attorneys found evidence the site appeared to be in the process of shaking down real estate agents for cash to get reviews of questionable origin removed from the site." In other words, it appears that false reviews were being created and then agents were being contacted and charged money to have certain reviews removed.

Some sites are at least honest enough to alert you to the potential for

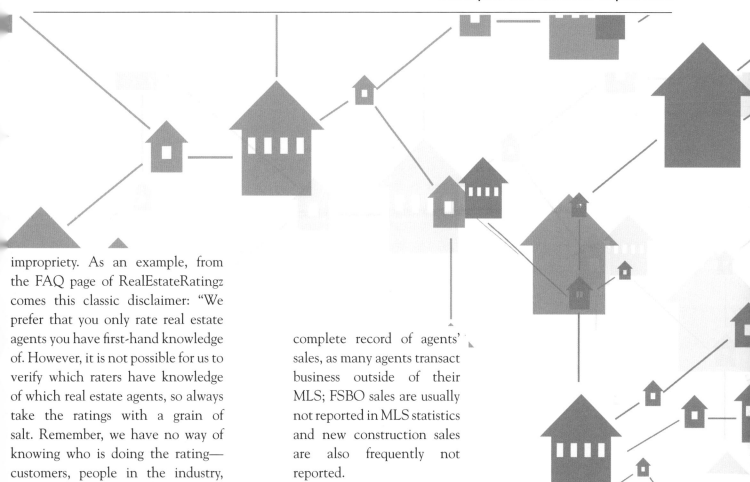

impropriety. As an example, from the FAQ page of RealEstateRatingz comes this classic disclaimer: "We prefer that you only rate real estate agents you have first-hand knowledge of. However, it is not possible for us to verify which raters have knowledge of which real estate agents, so always take the ratings with a grain of salt. Remember, we have no way of knowing who is doing the rating—customers, people in the industry, regular people, dogs, cats, etc."

This again underscores the wide range of efforts being made by online review sites to ensure—or not ensure—the veracity of the information they're sharing with the world.

MLS Challenges

Yet another factor to consider is the sites that use a philosophy we'll summarize as "the agent who sells the most is the best agent." The potential weaknesses with this approach are:

- There is not necessarily a correlation between volume of sales and quality of agent.

- Not all MLSs share information with all ratings sites.

- MLSs do not typically contain a 100 percent

complete record of agents' sales, as many agents transact business outside of their MLS; FSBO sales are usually not reported in MLS statistics and new construction sales are also frequently not reported.

As an illustration of what can happen when organizations attempt to leverage this incomplete MLS data to publicly rate agents, Redfin (redfin.com) aborted its MLS-based "Scouting Report" concept.

As reported in Inman News on October 4, 2011: "Seattle-based brokerage Redfin has pulled the plug on agent "Scouting Reports" it rolled out last week in 14 markets and part of Atlanta, saying there are inherent problems in the multiple listing service data the reports were based on that weren't easy to fix. Holes in the data—often created when agents work informally in teams, or don't inform the MLS when an out-of-town agent represented a buyer in a deal—meant that consumers weren't always getting the complete deal history

and performance metrics for every real estate agent, Redfin CEO Glenn Kelman said in a blog post. "Only a tiny fraction of transactions weren't accounted for, but it would have been enough to destroy our credibility if we had insisted on keeping Scouting Report live," Kelman wrote in an email to company employees reposted on the company's blog. "Had the data been accurate we'd have defended ourselves from MLS and agent complaints till hell froze over, but in the absence of accuracy we have no defense.""

Newer player HomeLight has dealt with this issue in a different way, as several MLSs refused to syndicate to their site. As reported in Inman News on December 5, 2012: "At the behest of a local California REALTOR®

association, the recently launched agent matching site HomeLight has pulled multiple listing service data from a Central Coast MLS previously displayed on the site. The move follows a similar request from the Kirkland, Washington-based Northwest Multiple Listing Service (NWMLS) last week."

It would appear that any agent rating site that bases its value proposition on MLS-sourced data will continue

will see when they search your name. Remember, in today's Internet-driven world, most potential clients and even other business contacts will most likely Google you at some point, so you may as well do all you can to maximize the "good" and to minimize the "bad" that shows up in these searches.

2. Create Google Alerts

Another thing we recommend you do is to create Google Alerts (google.

misspellings).

- The name of your brokerage, company and/or franchise.

- The key members of your team.

- Your largest competitors.

3. Deal with Negative Review

The last thing anyone wants to see is a negative review, but with easy access

to face challenges in the future.

MONITOR ONLINE REPUTATION

By establishing a few simple protocols you can easily stay abreast of what's being said about you online. This alone is a big step forward toward optimizing your online reputation.

1. Google Yourself

One of the first things you should do is enter your name and company into the search box on Google. "Googling yourself" will show you what others

com/alerts) for yourself. Google Alerts is a service that emails you whenever any term or phrase or search string that you specify appears on the Internet. Doing this is easy and this will keep you updated on anything that might find its way onto the web about you, your service or any other search you may create. You can elect to be "alerted" as search queries are found immediately, daily or weekly. Common Google Alerts you might create for yourself are:

- Your name (even consider

to the Internet and with so many sites having no barriers to consumers leaving feedback, it sometimes happens to honest agents. If you do receive a negative review, here's what we recommend you do:

- **Never Ignore It.** Negative reviews usually don't go away by themselves and often get worse if not addressed.

- **Respond Quickly.** One thing we've observed over and over is the reality of "the mob mentality" online. For better or worse, fair or unfair, it's a reality. When people react to criticism quickly, objectively and maturely, it very often diffuses the potential for additional negative comments.

- **Don't React Defensively.** Human nature is to react negatively to criticism. Avoid this if at all possible. Even if your critic has treated you unfairly, respond with maturity, objectivity and an open mind.

- **Don't Brawl.** As Mark Twain said it, "Never argue with a fool, onlookers may not be able to tell the difference."

- **Try to Take it Offline.** If you can get the critic to agree to discuss the matter privately—by phone or email—that's certainly preferable to hashing it out publicly.

- **Learn the Lesson.** It goes without saying; learn whatever lesson you can from the experience.

We've seen a number of situations where a harsh online critique was removed by the critic simply because the criticized party kept their composure, didn't react defensively and truly sought to understand the critic's point of view. In extreme cases, where a harsh critic won't come around, if you don't have the ability to remove or correct the review, try to reach the website provider

or company to determine the best course of action.

BEST PRACTICES
1. Complete Your Profiles
Take time to create and/or update profiles everywhere. You should at the very least have a complete and solid profile on Zillow, Trulia, Realtor.com and Google Plus Local. You should also make sure that the photo you use as your image/avatar is used consistently on social sites such as Facebook, Twitter or LinkedIn, as well as any personal websites or blogs where people might find you.

2. Optimize Your "About Me" Page
As noted in Chapter 1 on Blogging, on a typical website the second or third most visited page is "About Me." Many agents miss out on an opportunity to leverage this knowledge into making a great first impression on visitors. We recommend that you include Information about your client service philosophy, written and video testimonials and of course your contact information. Since you know you're going to have relatively high web traffic on this page, use that knowledge and lead with your best and most powerful reputation-enhancing content.

3. Leverage Social Media
Social Media platforms in general, and Facebook and Twitter in particular, are great places to:

- Demonstrate expertise.
- Syndicate success stories.
- Syndicate written testimonials.
- Syndicate video testimonials.

- Expand your reach.
- Connect with potential new clients.
- Build top-of-mind awareness.

Pacinelli reinforces this point by saying, "Online reputation is not just what people find on agent review sites, obviously. It's a sum total of your connections online. Your friends and followers increase your chances of being referred by someone. That is, the more legitimate friends you have online, the greater the chances that those friends will refer business to you."

This perspective is consistent with what we said earlier in this chapter, when we noted that the number one way both buyers and sellers find their agent is by referral from a friend, relative or neighbor.

4. Get Testimonials
For agents looking to maximize their online reputations, having as many quality testimonials as possible is crucial. The logical time to ask for a recommendation or testimonial is probably at the successful conclusion of a transaction, but it might be even better to ask for it at the initial meeting with the client. This can help to set the expectations so once the closing occurs it will seem like a normal extension of the process.

We suggest that your clients visit one of the sites mentioned above, or you can send them a direct request from one of the widgets built into a number of the review sites. Video reviews are becoming more and more powerful with the increase in traffic to sites like YouTube and Vimeo. Seek opportunities to get your client's testimonial or review on film. It's easy with today's mobile devices and tablets having powerful and easy-to-use video cameras. A nice aspect of video testimonials is that viewers can see the genuine emotion in the words and body language of the person sharing the feedback.

Cyndee Haydon, a real estate agent based in Clearwater Beach, Florida, has over 380 videos on her YouTube Channel, many of which are powerful testimonials. With over 185,000 video views, there's no doubt that some of Cyndee's clients have contacted her as a result of seeing other client comments. And DreamTown (dreamtown.com), a brokerage based in Chicago, features over 1,600 client testimonials, many of which are also video.

5. Syndicate Testimonials

Once you have testimonials and positive reviews, you will want to leverage them as many places as you can. You can do this in a variety of ways, but we'll sum it up by saying "syndicate them everywhere," including You Tube, your website, your blog, Facebook and Twitter. SocialBios is a tool that can help with this, and if dealing with videos, once they're uploaded to YouTube (or a similar video sharing site) they can be shared with social networks or embedded into blogs or websites with some simple "cutting and pasting" of HTML code.

6. Leverage Yelp

To illustrate the significance of Yelp, if you have an iPhone, do a search using Siri and ask this question:

"Find me a real estate agent in [name of your town]." If you do, Siri will respond with something about like this: "I found 15 real estate agents, 9 of whom are close to you. I've sorted them by ratings…" You certainly caught that last part! But where does Siri get those ratings? Yelp. This underscores why it's so important to have Yelp as one of the sites where you're building a body of positive testimonials from your clients.

SUMMARY

People love affirmation. They seek to get it from people and they look for opportunities to give it to others. We love getting comments and @ replies on Social Media and we give away our "Likes" and +1's and RTs as freely as we leave pennies in the cup at the convenience store counter. Need one? Take one. Have one? Leave one. But are they worth only a penny, or do they have a larger impact?

It can also make you feel good to warn someone not to waste their time, money or risk their health with something that you didn't enjoy. Being at the receiving end of a bad experience or wasting your time reading a horrible book may give you the motive to publicly criticize the provider and/or author.

And Social Media has effectively given everyone a microphone, a soapbox, a platform and a stage. We can all share our opinions on just about everything now. And, as the explosion of the popularity of Facebook and Twitter shows, more and more people are flocking to places where they can connect with others to share opinions and thoughts

on everything under the sun.

Online reputation isn't going away. On the contrary, it appears to be blossoming. So, the key is to get started as quickly as possible in managing your online reputation. Seek to create a significant and uniform positive body of content across as many online platforms that are appropriate and that you can manage effectively. Always provide remarkable service, treat others with courtesy and respect and follow the "under promise and over deliver" philosophy.

How To Become A Major Influencer Online
Klout: The Inside Track to Social Scoring

6

How To Become A Major Influencer Online

The British were coming! The plan was set. William Dawes mounted his horse and rode off into the darkness to warn everyone along the Massachusetts countryside on his way to Lexington. Now some of you are probably wondering why our recollection of the events of April 18, 1775 is slightly off. You might be wondering exactly who this William Dawes impostor might be. Yes, Paul Revere was the rider who warned his fellow countrymen that the British were coming; that much is true and historical fact. However, it's worth exploring the story of his lesser-known counterpart, William Dawes, to illustrate the importance of perceived social influence. History remembers the influencer.

In his bestselling book *The Tipping Point*, Malcolm Gladwell explored the difference between these two riders. His conclusion? Revere was a "connector" while Dawes was not. Said another way, Revere had influence and he knew who was influential at each of his stops as he made his way to Lexington. Revere had spent time building a network of influencers prior to his night ride, while it would appear that Dawes had not. This in fact made Revere's message more effective along his route, but it also helped him to arrive in Lexington well before Dawes completed his ride. Dawes simply warned whomever he could find in each of his stops and the rest, as they say, is history.

Revere's place in the annals of history clearly demonstrates that his word of mouth warning had a significant impact in the American Revolution. Gladwell summarized the importance of word of mouth this way:

"Word of mouth is—even in this age of mass communications and multimillion dollar advertising campaigns—still the most important form of human communication. Think, for a moment, about the least expensive restaurant you went to, the last expensive piece of clothing you bought and the last movie you saw. In how many of those cases was your decision about where to spend your money heavily influenced by the recommendation of a friend? There are plenty of advertising executives who think that precisely because of the sheer ubiquity of marketing efforts these days, word of mouth appeals have become the only kind of persuasion that most of us respond to anymore."

THE INFLUENCE REVOLUTION

While the British aren't coming any longer and you certainly wouldn't hop on a steed in this day and age to spread your message, the lesson of Revere's influence is still as important right now as it was on that historic night 238 years ago. Influence certainly matters in today's world, where digital and Social Media have combined to create a new type of revolution. Let's take a look at some examples of this "influence revolution" and how some organizations and individuals are leveraging this paradigm.

Virgin America

Virgin America was launching a new route. Instead of

their usual, traditional marketing strategy, they reached out via Klout (klout.com) to identify influencers. "We offered 120 free flights for this campaign—all of which were booked within a matter of weeks—so we were very pleased with how much enthusiasm was generated to take advantage of our offer," said Porter Gale, vice president of marketing at Virgin, cited in AdAge. "We saw a ton of Social Media buzz and press around the campaign, which definitely helped to build awareness for our brand and product." The campaign garnered coverage in top blogs and news outlets, resulting in over 7.4 million impressions (the number of times content is displayed for consumption).

Calvin Lee

One person on that Virgin flight was Calvin Lee. You might not recognize the name, but many companies are actively seeking Calvin in hopes that he will tweet about their products. Why? He has almost 80,000 followers on Twitter and a Klout score of 70. When he tweets, his followers listen, but more importantly, they engage. Besides flying on Virgin, Calvin has done car and product test-drives, been invited to cover events from the "average Joe's" point of view and the list of his perks just keeps growing. What's most fascinating about Calvin is the fact that he really isn't anyone special; he's just a graphic designer who built a large following from scratch.

Robert Scoble

Prior to joining Microsoft in 2003 where he created videos showcasing their products, Robert Scoble had

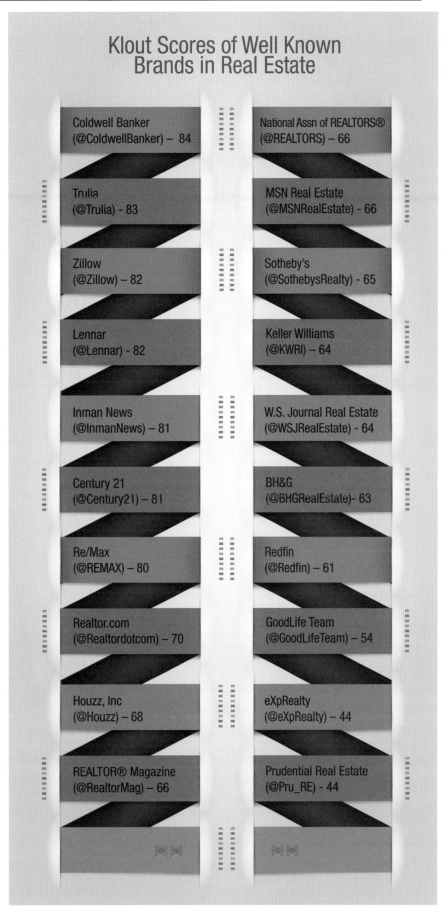

Klout Scores of Well Known Brands in Real Estate

Coldwell Banker (@ColdwellBanker) – 84

Trulia (@Trulia) - 83

Zillow (@Zillow) – 82

Lennar (@Lennar) - 82

Inman News (@InmanNews) – 81

Century 21 (@Century21) – 81

Re/Max (@REMAX) – 80

Realtor.com (@Realtordotcom) – 70

Houzz, Inc (@Houzz) – 68

REALTOR® Magazine (@RealtorMag) – 66

National Assn of REALTORS® (@REALTORS) – 66

MSN Real Estate (@MSNRealEstate) - 66

Sotheby's (@SothebysRealty) - 65

Keller Williams (@KWRI) – 64

W.S. Journal Real Estate (@WSJRealEstate) - 64

BH&G (@BHGRealEstate)- 63

Redfin (@Redfin) – 61

GoodLife Team (@GoodLifeTeam) – 54

eXpRealty (@eXpRealty) – 44

Prudential Real Estate (@Pru_RE) - 44

SOURCE CROWD SOURCED BY MICHAEL MCCLURE FEB 2012

worked in a San Jose camera shop and in various video production

for the first time made tangible, quantified, summarized and presented

various Social Media platforms/ profiles to which a user grants Klout

Word of mouth is—even in this age of mass communications and multimillion dollar advertising campaigns—still the most important form of human communication.

companies. His work at Microsoft quickly catapulted him to fame and he became quite possibly the world's first professional "spokesblogger." In 2006 he left Microsoft and became a very sought after speaker as his influence continued to grow. The pinnacle of his influence manifested during the 2010 - 2011 holiday season when he posted a blog titled "Is Quora the Biggest Blogging Innovation in 10 Years?" Website traffic was increased by nearly 400 percent in the week following his post. One man, purely because of his personal influence, created the equivalent of winning the online lottery for one company—in terms of website visitors—by simply writing a blog post.

ABOUT KLOUT
1. The Challenge
Since the beginning of time, influence has existed as humans have interacted with one another. The challenge comes in quantifying this influence. Clearly, one person can have more influence than another, but how can that be effectively measured? The consideration of measuring one's relative clout became even more intriguing and complicated with the advent of the Social Media era, as "friend" and "follower" counts were

publicly for all to see. This dilemma, or perhaps we should say opportunity, is exactly what inspired co-founders Joe Fernandez and Binh Tran to launch Klout in 2007.

2. A Brief History
Klout started its work of measuring Social Media influence with the Twitter platform. They ran their first "perk" with Starbucks in March 2010 and added the Facebook social network later that year. 2011 was a very busy year as they added several more networks, raised some serious capital and became the launching pad for Spotify (spotify.com). In September 2011, Klout celebrated 100 million scores calculated.

While there are other social scoring platforms available to users, Klout has emerged as the de facto "Standard for Influence" in today's Social Media realm.

3. What Does it Measure?
Klout measures influence across the

access. The score is based on the interactions, conversations and social actions a user drives via Facebook Likes, Facebook shares, Twitter retweets, etc. The scoring ranges from 1 to 100, with 40 marking the current average score among all Klout users. While the exact algorithm is a closely guarded secret, the following is outlined on the Klout website: "The science behind the score examines more than 400 variables on multiple social networks beyond your number of followers and friends. It looks at who is engaging with your content and who they are sharing it with."

Another important aspect of the score is the "ratio effect" of a user's

online activities. If a user tweets 100 times and generates 1,000 Retweets that will affect the user's Klout score more profoundly than 1,000 tweets that generate 100 Retweets. Another interesting factor is the selectivity of the people interacting with a user's content. For example, on Facebook if

one person likes 10 of a user's posts in one day, that isn't weighted the same as 10 different people liking just one of a user's posts. In fact, if the same person interacts with multiple pieces of a user's content in the same day, the incremental weight assigned by Klout to each of those successive interactions will decline. Klout also looks for inauthentic behaviors to help ensure the accuracy and integrity of the score. Users will notice regular updates to the algorithm by Klout, as they continually seek to improve the accuracy and integrity of the scoring, especially as they add more networks.

4. The Scores

How does Klout make sense of all of this data and present it for users to understand? Their layout and visualization of a user's score gives users a quick snapshot of what's happening across their linked networks. A user's Klout score is identified in the top left corner in Klout's distinctive orange box. Outside programs, such as Hootsuite, can automatically import and display a user's Klout score in the user's profile on those external platforms. Directly adjacent to the Klout score is the profile image the user selected. This is generally a Twitter or Facebook profile picture, depending on which the user selected during setup, or it can be some other image that is specific to Klout that the user selected. A user's linked accounts will then be displayed in color to the right of their Klout score and picture. The accounts in color indicate an active linked account, while the black and white icons illustrate those accounts that are not connected.

5. Dashboard

The graph located below the Klout score, picture and linked accounts is a representation of the score's 90-day history. Generally, scores will not fluctuate much from day-to-day. To the right of the graph is a quick snapshot of what a user's score did in the last 24 hours, indicating an up or down change and daily score differential. Below that are seven-day, 30-day and 90-day score changes. This gives a user a quick, easy look to see if they are improving or going backward in terms of their Social Media interaction and engagement efforts.

Top 100 Klout Scores of Individuals in Real Estate

Stefan Swanepoel (@Swanepoel)	79
Rebekah Radice (@RebekahRadice)	78
Michael McClure (@ProfessionalOne)	77
Chris Smith (@Chris_Smth)	77
Kelly Mitchell (@KellyMitchell)	77
Katie Lance (@KatieLance)	77
Cyndee Haydon (@CyndeeHaydon)	76
Nicole Nicolay (@Nik_Nik)	76
Jay Papasan (@JayPapasan)	76
Laurie Davis (@LaurieWDavis)	76
Chad Hyams (@ChadHyams)	76
Sean Carpenter (@SeanCarp)	75
Jay Thompson (@PhxREguy)	75
Laura Monroe (@LauraMonroe)	75
Albie Vas (@AblieVas)	75
Lori Ballen (@BallenGroup)	75
Joe Winpisinger (@3rdWAVElands)	74
Aaron Kaufman (@AaronKaufman)	74
Matthew Shadbolt (@Corcoran_Group)	74

Paula Henry (@IndyAgent)	74
Patricia Young (@PatriciaAYoung)	74
Cyndi Carfrey (@KWCyndi)	73
Sherry Chris (@SherryChris)	73
David Patterson (@ibdp3)	73
Jimmy Mackin (@JimmyMackin)	72
Jared James (@JaredJamesToday)	72
Axay Parekh (@Axtulsa)	72
Bill Gassett (@MassRealty)	72
Kevin Kauffman (@KevinKauffman9)	72
Jeff Chalmers (@ClicknFinance)	72
Liz Landry (@Liz_Landry)	72
Janie Coffey (@JanieC)	71
Bill Lublin (@BillLublin)	71
Paua Mosley (@PaulaMosley)	71
Jeff Lobb (@JeffLobb)	71
Marc Davison (@1000WattMarc)	71
Sheila Cuadros (@SheilaCuadros)	71
Ines Hegedus-Garcia (@Ines)	71

Janice Baldwin (@JanieBaldwinKW)	71
Seth Campbell (@SethCampbell)	71
KevinTomlinson (@MiamiBeach)	70
Christy Grossman (@TheBeltTeam)	70
Stephanie Chumbley (@DepModeChick)	70
Jennifer Branchini (@49ersCam)	70
Sue Adler (@SueAdler)	70
Gerard Dunn (@PotomacSecret)	70

Amy Chorew (@AmyChorew)	70
Richard Silver (@RichardSilver)	70
Tom Ferry (@CoachTomFerry)	70
Debra Trappen (@Debra11)	70
Keith Grogan (@SellTeam)	70
Tim Davis (@TimDavisOnline)	70
Chris Alston (Chris_Alston)	70
Lisa Archer (@LisaArcher)	69

Nobu Hata (@NobuHata)	69
Christophe Choo (@ChristopheChoo)	69
Heather Elias (@LocoHeather)	69
Kelley Skar (@KelleySkar)	69
Mike Bowler (@MIRealEstate)	69
Steve Schrader Bachar (@MRSteveSB)	69
Michael Maher (@7LBook)	69
Katie Jones (@KatieJones_KW)	69
Patrick Healy (@PatrickHealy)	69
Debbie Kirkland (@FloridaSunSales)	69
Dawn Rose (@DawnRoseRealty)	69
Virginia Munden (@VirginiaMunden)	68
Bobbi Howe (@BobbiHowe)	68
Chris Griffith (@ChrisGriffithFL)	68
Lani Rosales (@LaniAR)	68
Jim Marks (@JimMarks)	68
Joshua Dorkin (@JRDorkin)	68
Herman Chan (@Hermanity)	68
Mariana Wagner (@Mizzle)	68
Patrick Woods (@PWWoods)	68

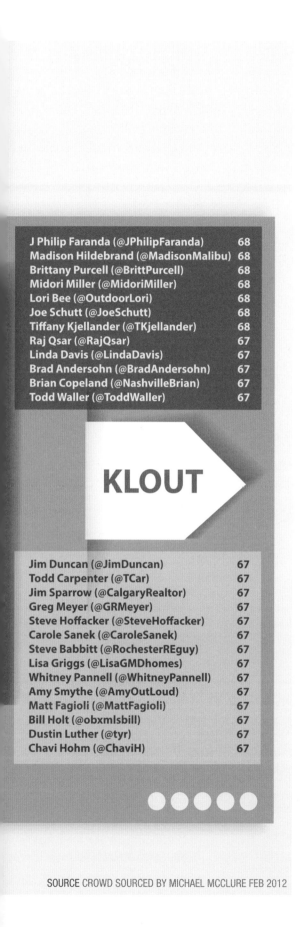

J Philip Faranda (@JPhilipFaranda)	68
Madison Hildebrand (@MadisonMalibu)	68
Brittany Purcell (@BrittPurcell)	68
Midori Miller (@MidoriMiller)	68
Lori Bee (@OutdoorLori)	68
Joe Schutt (@JoeSchutt)	68
Tiffany Kjellander (@TKjellander)	68
Raj Qsar (@RajQsar)	67
Linda Davis (@LindaDavis)	67
Brad Andersohn (@BradAndersohn)	67
Brian Copeland (@NashvilleBrian)	67
Todd Waller (@ToddWaller)	67

KLOUT

Jim Duncan (@JimDuncan)	67
Todd Carpenter (@TCar)	67
Jim Sparrow (@CalgaryRealtor)	67
Greg Meyer (@GRMeyer)	67
Steve Hoffacker (@SteveHoffacker)	67
Carole Sanek (@CaroleSanek)	67
Steve Babbitt (@RochesterREguy)	67
Lisa Griggs (@LisaGMDhomes)	67
Whitney Pannell (@WhitneyPannell)	67
Amy Smythe (@AmyOutLoud)	67
Matt Fagioli (@MattFagioli)	67
Bill Holt (@obxmlsbill)	67
Dustin Luther (@tyr)	67
Chavi Hohm (@ChaviH)	67

The circle graph below the 90-day graph is a representation of how the different linked social networks contribute to a user's score. In the example, you will notice that this user's score is comprised mostly of Twitter and Facebook interactions, and that Facebook accounts for 53 percent of the overall Klout score. To the right of this circle graph is displayed important data that is collected from each of the connected social networks. This data includes several of the measured signals discussed earlier.

Recently, Klout added "top social interactions over the past 90-days" to their dashboard display. This gives the user a unique insight into what posts have had the greatest impact on their score. More importantly, they give a user an invaluable glimpse into the type of content they created that "worked" in terms of building positive influence, engagement and interaction.

Another valuable aspect of this display of top interactions is the inclusion of the actual interactions to the right of the original post. This feature is a great tool for a user to leverage. With most interactions you can see who liked, commented or Retweeted within the originating platform. They

have also made it easier for a user to identify the most effective posts with their "five-dot indicator" in the upper right corner of the original post, with five green dots highlighting the posts that have created most interaction.

6. Your Influencers

Within the Klout profile page, located directly below the profile information, you will find a list of a user's top influencers. These are listed from highest score down. To see more influencers, simply mouse over to the right of the "Your Influencers" title and a "see more" option will appear. This feature helps users to identify the key influencers they engage with most. It can give a user valuable insight into how they affect both the user's score and their Social Media interactions. If you click on the "see more" option, a new screen will display top influencers and also identify the top three topics for each. These topics will help a user understand how these people influence them and give them the option to reward them with +K for the interactions they've had with them.

7. Topics and +K

While a user's overall score is the focus of Klout, the addition of topics and +K to the user profile made the platform an even more useful tool. In the process of gathering the data to create its score, Klout is able to identify the topics about which a user has the most influence. In addition to identifying these topics, fellow users have the ability to award +K, similar to Google+'s +1, to the people who influence them on particular topics. As mentioned earlier, +K is one of the signals that the company uses to compute a user's overall score. +K's are important because other users are identifying a user as influential to

them on that particular topic. When a user receives +K from another Klout user, it is instant and meaningful feedback that their Social Media efforts are paying dividends and having an impact. If your topics and +K's aren't in line with your Social Media content strategy, then you have some work to do on tweaking your posts.

Another benefit of topics and +K is the ability to locate, follow and

engage with influential people on the subjects that matter the most to you. Doing so will help you by adding valuable content to potentially fuel your content curation efforts, and also providing additional opportunity to engage with these people and improve your own score.

8. Klout Perks

Clearly there is a social influence benefit to linking your various Social Media accounts and improving your social scoring. Klout, however, has taken this idea one step further by implementing a program of perks available to influencers based on their topics and score. The program offers companies the opportunity to identify and offer their products to these influencers.

Most perks are based on your score in relation to the topics you're influential about. Users with influence in the topic of video were recently treated to free flipcams. RedBull recently sent four-packs of their product to influencers on a variety of topics.

KLOUT'S CORE CONCEPTS

To summarize, Klout believes in these six core concepts as stated on their website:

1. Connecting Networks Can Only Help Your Score.

We want to help you understand your influence wherever it may exist. We also understand, given the number of different

Top Real Estate Influencers

SOURCE KLOUT

networks out there, that it is nearly impossible for any person to be consistently effective across every network. Adding more networks helps us more accurately measure your influence and can only increase your Score.

are, the greater impact you have. All engagement positively contributes to your Score.

5. Klout is Constantly Evolving.

The social web is changing every day and the Klout score will continue

> ## Just because such "social scoring" hasn't had a direct impact on your financial bottom line today doesn't mean it's never going to happen.

2. Influence is Built Over Time.

In most instances, your influence should not radically change from one day to the next. Your score is based on a rolling 90-day window, with recent activity being weighted more than older activity. Being inactive over the weekend or taking a short break won't have a major impact on your Score, but if you're inactive for longer periods your Score will decrease gradually.

3. Influence is the Ability to Drive Action.

It's great to have lots of connections, but what really matters is how people engage with the content you create. We believe it's better to have a small and engaged audience than a large network that doesn't actively respond to your content.

4. Everyone has Klout.

You are never penalized for connecting or engaging with someone with a low score. In fact, you are helping build their score. The more influential you

to evolve and improve. The best strategy for obtaining a high Klout score is to simply create great content that your network wants to share and engage with.

6. Being Active is Different than Being Influential.

Retweets, Likes, comments and other interactions on the social web are all signals of influence. However, just looking at the count of these actions doesn't tell the whole story of a person's influence. It's important to look at how much content a person creates compared to the amount of engagement they generate.

SHOULD SOCIAL SCORING MATTER?

Understanding what Klout is and how it works is just part of the equation. Knowing why it matters and how it could impact you is the next step. In April 2012 Wired Magazine's (wired. com) Seth Stevenson related the following story:

"Last spring Sam Fiorella was recruited for a VP position at a large Toronto marketing agency. With 15 years of experience consulting for major brands like AOL, Ford and Kraft, Fiorella felt confident in his qualifications. But midway through the interview, he was caught off guard when his interviewer asked him for his Klout score. Fiorella hesitated awkwardly before confessing that he had no idea what a Klout score was. The interviewer pulled up the webpage for Klout. com—a service that purports to measure users' online influence on a scale from 1 to 100—and angled the monitor so that Fiorella could see the humbling result for himself: His score was 34. "He cut the interview short pretty soon after that," Fiorella says. Later he learned that he'd been eliminated as a candidate specifically because his Klout score was too low. "They hired a guy whose score was 67.""

Partly intrigued, partly scared, Fiorella spent the next six months working feverishly to boost his Klout score, eventually hitting 72. As his score rose, so did the number of job offers and speaking invitations he received. "Fifteen years of accomplishments weren't as important as that score," he says." Given Stevenson's example of Fiorella's experience, is it really too much of a stretch to see potential real estate clients one day looking up your Klout score and comparing it with that of other real estate professionals they're interviewing?

From the Vault: Real Estate Confronts Reality (1997)

"Soon the consumer will be able to go to many different sources for that information. The era of unlimited access to information is now upon us, and the data the industry covered so long now has no exclusive value."

Not only that, but keep this in mind: we are on the early, cutting edge of these kinds of analytics having real impact on real world decisions. Just because such "social scoring" hasn't had a direct impact on your financial bottom line today doesn't mean it's never going to happen.

Companies are taking note of social scoring in general and Klout in particular and its impact on social influence. They are giving preferential treatment to those with higher scores, with the expectation that it will result in Social Media interactions that will benefit their company or product.

As another example, not long ago the Palms Casino in Las Vegas implemented a social strategy of upgrading guests with high Klout scores. Prior to this strategy the Palms was ranked 17th among all of the Vegas hotel-casinos in terms of Social Media followers. This plan created tremendous online buzz and as influencers began to share their Palms experience with their Social Media audiences, they elevated the Palms' standing on Facebook. They now have one of the highest Klout scores among their competitors. Not bad for a boutique (non-chain) casino in Las Vegas.

The Klout phenomenon has also bled over into customer service. While most companies will not admit that they give preferential treatment to those with high Klout scores, it's interesting to note how many of them are using a new tool from Salesforce (salesforce.com). This tool helps companies monitor online comments made about their company, product or service based upon the commenter's Klout score, thus giving higher credence to complaints or comments from the most influential people. While Salesforce doesn't tell the companies how to treat these people, they do help identify the ones that they should be paying attention to the most.

INFLUENCERS IN REAL ESTATE

In this chapter we have presented three lists of influencers in real estate:

- The first is comprised of the major brands and other significant entities in the real estate space ranked by their Klout scores.

- represents the "Top 100

- The second list individual Klout scores" that we could find in the industry. We used a variety of resources to assemble this list as Klout does not allow for perfect

searching in the manner we intended; our list is therefore subjective. The list represents one hundred individuals we located in or peripheral to the real estate industry with the highest Klout scores.

- The third list is what Klout itself shows as the "Top Real Estate Influencers." This is simply a list of what Klout displays when you click on the specific topic "real estate." It's our understanding that this likely represents the brands, companies and individuals who have received the most +Ks on the specific topic of "real estate."

MAXIMIZING YOUR KLOUT

If you refer back to the list of signals measured by Klout, you'll remember that the number of followers, friends, etc. is not weighted the same as interactions and engagements with the followers you actually have. To put it another way, someone with 50,000 Twitter followers—but who isn't that great at engaging with others—can actually have a lower score than someone with only 900 actively engaged followers. It's what you do with the followers you have that matters more than the total number. Chris Makarsky, product director at Klout, offers a few suggestions on things you should focus on to improve your score:

- Improve the cadence, or frequency, of your Social Media posts. Obviously more posts provide the opportunity for more interaction and engagement. But a balance must be struck so as not to turn off your following with "over sharing."

- Focus on fewer topics and don't spread yourself thin. This is an easy suggestion for real estate professionals, as they tend to focus their attention on the industry. But you should beware of becoming one-dimensional

- Be positive, as positive interactions tend to drive higher levels of engagement than negative.

WHAT'S NEXT?

At this point, it seems to be the general consensus that Klout is the leader in terms of social scoring concepts. It's also safe to assume that they will continue to tweak, adjust and improve their algorithm as new social platforms emerge and evolve. It's rumored that they recently secured $40 Million in funding from various top venture capital leaders, including Microsoft, which now adds a person's Klout score to their profile in Bing (bing.com) social search bar results. According to public data

add a "where a person is influential" factor into their algorithm as well.

It will also be interesting to see how, or if, Klout can incorporate real life influence. It has been criticized for its low scoring of offline influencers such as Oprah and Malcolm Gladwell, who aren't active on Social Media sites. The addition of Wikipedia pages to their algorithm has helped to add real world influence, but there is still much room for improvement. This will be a discussion worth following over the next several years as the debate continues regarding offline versus online influence.

Another insight into where Klout might be heading can be summarized

> A high IQ usually points to a smarter person. A high Klout score usually points to a person who is active online. It's neither good nor bad. It just is.

as well, by mixing in at least two other non-industry-specific topics like food, travel, etc.

- Engage with those who have high scores. An RT (retweet), Like or comment from someone with a higher score carries more weight than one from someone with a lower score. Is this an edict to ignore those with lower scores? Not at all! All engagement and interactions help your score, some more than others though.

and estimates, Klout receives more hits to its application programming interface (API) from third-party applications than all social scoring type companies combined.

As hyper-localism and geo-location become increasingly more valuable in both Social Media and real estate, it's logical to assume that Klout will begin focusing on local influence versus global influence. Their focus on topics and +K was the first step in that direction, helping a user see what they are influential about. It makes sense to assume that Klout would at some point focus on geography to

in this statement from founder Joe Fernandez: "Rather than thinking of Klout as a grading system, Klout should expose the world to what you're passionate about or an expert about. Use Klout to help you curate that and show it to the world to benefit you and beyond. How does your Klout score fade to the background and how does what you're doing with your influence become most important?"

OTHER PLATFORMS

Other platforms that also measure social influence and provide valuable insights are (in alphabetical order):

1. Empire Avenue

Empire Avenue (empireavenue.com) turns the social influence measurement issue into more of a game. Think of it as a stock market for your social profile, where users can buy and sell shares in their friends' Empire Avenue accounts. They definitely win the award for incorporating a gaming element when it comes to social scoring.

2. Kred

This site (kred.com) takes more of a Flipboard approach, with a focus on the visualization of your influence. Explore the posts, pictures and links that make you influential. See your full influence story and zoom in on meaningful moments.

3. Peer Index

This site assigns you a score on a scale of 1 to 100 based on their algorithm, which analyzes data from social platforms to which you grant access. One interesting tool is the comparison of your score to that of those you recently conversed with online.

4. PROskore

This is an online business network (proskore.com) aimed at measuring your professional reputation. Think LinkedIn and Klout combined.

5. SocMetrics

This site (socmetrics.com) focuses their efforts on identifying influencers on specific topics. You can search and filter influencers based on topic and location.

6. Social Mention

This site (socialmention.com) offers real-time Social Media search and analysis. Think Google Alerts, but for Social Media. While not a social scoring site, SocialMention offers very useful statistics to help your Social Media efforts.

7. Tweet Grader (aka Twitter Grader)

This site (tweet.grader.com) scores your Twitter profile between 1 and 100. In addition, they offer suggestions and tips to improve your Twitter presence. The site also ranks you among all users, users in your state and even within your home city.

8. Twenty Feet

Twenty Feet (twentyfeet.com) is very much an analytical tool. They scrub data from your social profiles and give it to you in an assortment of graphs. While not necessarily a rating site, Twenty Feet provides some powerful data tied with email notifications based on your preferences.

SUMMARY

It's not that your Klout score matters per se, or that you should check it regularly. Similar to your IQ, or any other personality profile, scoring or measuring system, it is an indicator. It's not the number, but what the number represents and how you can use this additional information and knowledge to your advanrage.

Influencer Landscape

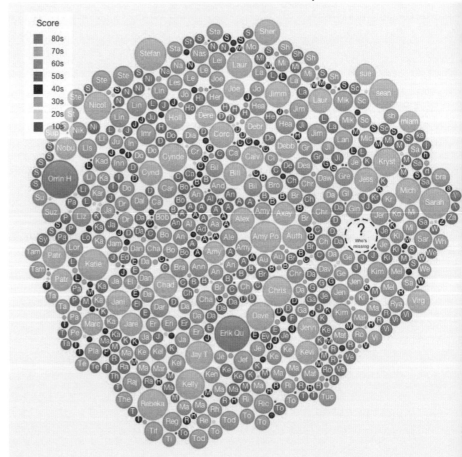

SOURCE KLOUT

A high IQ usually points to a smarter person. A high Klout score usually points to a person who is active online. It may be because the person blogs frequently, tweets a lot, is active on Facebook, participates in online groups extensively, etc. or a multitude of combinations thereof—the bottom line is that a higher score indicates that that person is more active, more pervasive and more well known online than someone with a lower score.

To become a major influencer online you must be cognizant of and seek to optimize your social scoring. Here are some steps to consider:

- Klout is already scoring you based on public postings they've accessed. Improve your score immediately by claiming your profile and connecting your networks. You do have the option to opt out of Klout, but we think that's not a wise move given the growing prevalence of social scoring.

- Use Klout topics and +K to fine tune and tweak your Social Media content strategy. Ensure that the topics you are rated on and the +Ks you receive are consistent with your messaging and objectives

- Create the "RITE" content. In his book *Return on Influence*, Mark Schaefer recommends this: "Focus on creating content that is RITE: relevant, interesting, timely and entertaining. If you consistently hold this filter up to any content you create, you'll be on your way to creating value that becomes part of the signal instead of the noise."

- Be authentic. While you might be able to game the system briefly, eventually it will catch up to you. Your online persona needs to match your offline one as well. The online community you operate in is much smaller than you might think. Over the long haul, being the authentic you is—by far—the most effective way to reach your potential in the online world.

- Don't get caught up in your score. If you're doing the right things the score will reflect that. Focus on executing the right actions—those that create positive engagement—and let the measurement of your efforts happen naturally and organically.

Our final advice: check your social scoring from time-to-time just to see how you're doing. While companies like Klout aren't perfect—no metric is—it can be a helpful way to determine if your Social Media efforts are or are not helping to boost your online influence. In a world where online influence matters more and more every day, we think that's a good habit to form.

7 The Ultimate Digital Organization System

Evernote: Systemize Your Entire Real Estate Business

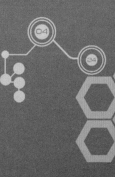

The Ultimate Digital Organization System

Evernote is a software platform designed for note taking, archiving, cloud storage and the sharing of information; it's designed to help you "remember everything." Evernote Notes can be a piece of text, a webpage, a portion of a webpage, a photograph, an audio message or anything that can be digitally scanned. Notes are stored in "Notebooks," which are essentially the digital equivalents of paper folders as you'd think of them in the physical world. They can be typed, dictated, edited, clipped, annotated, searched, exported and shared.

Because of the quality and the design of the Evernote (evernote.com) platform, as well as the overall value, utility and functionality of the software, it's often viewed as the ultimate digital organization and archiving system. The ability to store information "in the cloud" (on Evernote's servers and not necessarily on the user's computer, which can free up space) and access that information from anywhere across a wide range of operating systems and devices makes it a very powerful organization and productivity tool. With approximately 48M users as of January 2013—up from 25M in May of 2012—it's growing explosively on the strength of its overall value proposition. In fact, it's become so popular that some bookstores even have Evernote sections in them.

HOW IT WORKS

Evernote supports most every popular operating system, and it can be used in either desktop or web-based versions. However, when exclusively using the desktop software, you aren't able to upload files to the server or use the server to synchronize or share files on different devices,

which is one of the primary advantages of Evernote. Also, no image or PDF recognition and indexing are available in the desktop version. Our advice: use a combination of the desktop and web-based versions and regularly "sync" the two to ensure that all of your Notes are current and accessible from anywhere at any time.

Notes can be created a number of ways, including traditional keyboard entry, image capture from cameras on supported devices, by dragging and dropping files, images or blocks of text onto the Evernote icon on your desktop and by recording audio Notes. In some situations text that appears in captured images or in imported handwritten Notes can be recognized by using its Optical Character Recognition (OCR) technology. The Company has also

> **Evernote has become so popular that some bookstores even have Evernote sections in them.**

Remember everything.

Capture anything.
Save your ideas, things you like, things you hear, and things you see.

Access anywhere.
Evernote works with nearly every computer, phone and mobile device out there.

Find things fast.
Search by keyword, tag or even printed and handwritten text inside images.

SOURCE EVERNOTE

created "web clipper" plug-ins that can be used across a range of web browsers. These web clippers allow users to create Notes consisting of entire webpages or excerpted portions by simply clicking a button in a browser toolbar (more below).

Evernote also supports the ability to convert sent e-mails into Notes using an Evernote-specific e-mail address that is assigned to each user during the sign up process. When appropriate hardware is used the program can automatically add geo-tagging to Notes. With certain limitations, tweets can also be configured to automatically create Notes using specific "@" tagging within a tweet.

Notes can also be shared for viewing and editing by others if you're using the premium version. The free version has a monthly usage limitation of 60 MB/month. The premium version, which costs $5 per month or $45 per year, expands the usage limitation to 1,024 MB/month,

and it offers additional features. Both versions have an absolute limit of 100,000 notes and 250 Notebooks. Be aware that there are also minor variations in terms of the features that are available depending upon the platform/operating system being used.

BEST PRACTICES
1. Take Notes
Get in the habit of taking Notes on your computer, your Smartphone or your iPad. Notes are accessible from any web-enabled device at any time. They are indexable and keyword-and-tag searchable, making finding anything you've created an easy process. Enhanced search (premium version) uses OCR for reading PDFs and handwritten notes.

2. Travel Light
One of our favorite aspects of Evernote is that it allows you to "leave your laptop at home." It renders and performs beautifully on both Smartphones and tablets (the image

is from an iPad). Once you have most of your important documents loaded into Evernote you can travel lighter, using only your Smartphone or your tablet to access all your information. This is ideal for mobile professionals like real estate agents.

3. Create Primary Notebook Stacks
As already stated, Notebooks function exactly like manila folders do in the physical world. You can "stack" Notebooks within other Notebooks but this embedding is limited to "one level down." With that in mind, you should create separate Stacks for "My Listings," "My Buyers," "My Closed Sales" and "My Templates." These four Stacks will serve as the digital backbone of all of your real estate activities.

4. Create Templates
If you're not already using some sort of automated checklist as a transaction management tool (e.g. Top Producer), Evernote is a very serviceable option. Here's how:

- Identify every "repetitive process sequence" that you use in your business. Examples would be preparing for a listing appointment, doing a buyer consultation, doing home tours with buyers, obtaining a listing, managing a buyer-side sale from contract to close, managing a listing-side sale from contract to close, syndicating your listings, putting a listing in the MLS, etc.

Evernote Premium Features List

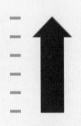
Supersized uploads
Evernote Premium boosts your monthly uploads to 1GB each month, enough to store high-res photos, lots of files, and thousands of text notes and web clips.

Top priority support
Have a question or problem? You'll be sent to the front of the queue for faster support response.

Offline notebooks
Take entire notebooks offline for easy access when you don't have a network connection. A perfect option for when you're traveling. Available on iOS and Android.

PDF search
Whenever you add a scanned document into your Evernote account, we'll make the PDF searchable so you can find it anytime.

Work together
Evernote Premium users can allow others to edit their notes, making Evernote a great tool for working on a project with others or planning a trip with friends.

Note history
Go back in time. View past versions of individual notes in your account. This is a great option when you're working with others.

Larger files, bigger notes
As a Premium user, the size of a single note is increased to 100MB. That means you can put more stuff into each of your notes.

Faster image recognition
Evernote makes images containing printed or handwritten text searchable. As a Premium user, your images get processed faster.

PIN lock
iOS and Android users can add a lock to their Evernote app for an extra level of security.

Hide promotions
Our promotions are designed to give you great ideas for using Evernote. If you prefer a distraction-free interface, you'll be able to easily hide the promotion box.

- For every sequence, create a "template" Note, which includes all of the steps that you normally complete during the respective sequence, and place each template in the Notebook called "My Templates."

- Every time you need one of these templates, go into your My Templates Notebook, find the template you want, copy the content, create a new Note in the applicable buyer or seller Notebook and paste the templated content into your new Note.

Over time, as you build your My Templates Notebook, you will enjoy substantial gains in productivity and efficiency as you perfect the population and composition of those templates. You'll never have to reinvent the wheel again.

5. Manage Listings
When it comes to working with listings, here are the individual Notes or items to consider including in the unique listing Notebook you create for each new selling client:

- Notes from your initial phone consultation.

- Pre-listing appointment notes.

- Copies of documents you obtained from local municipalities.

- PDFs you may have downloaded from municipality websites.

- Screen grabs you may have taken from municipality websites.

- Tax information.

- PDFs of comps.

- PDFs of CMAs.

- PDF of your seller's net sheet.

- Notes taken during your listing appointment.

- Room dimensions taken during your listing appointment.

- Audio notes taken while touring the home for the first time (see below for additional commentary on creating audio Notes).

- Your proposed listing description or narrative.

- Photos of the home.

- A copy of the listing agreement.

- A copy of the MLS input sheet.

- A copy of the brochure or other marketing materials you may have created for the listing.

- A copy of the disclosure documents relating to the listing.

- Copies of any updated CMAs you may send to the client following the inception of the listing.

- Copies of offers you may have received.

- A copy of the final contract when the property is ultimately sold.

- A copy of the closing documents.

6. Respond to Buyer Inquiries
With regard to your inventory of active listings, you should create a separate Note for each unique listing to send to potentially interested buyers. You can populate these Notes with only those items that are suitable for promotional purposes and for sharing with a potential buyer, e.g., a copy of the listing, a promotional brochure or literature you may have created, disclosures, etc.

This can be handy when someone calls with an inquiry about one of your listings. You can immediately open the applicable Note and share it using Evernote's email sharing functionality. This will save you time and create a great impression with the person with whom you're communicating.

We also recommend that you create a Notebook containing nothing but PDF copies of all of your listings. It's uncanny how often someone will have a question about one of your listings when you're on the road or in the middle of something else, when it's inconvenient for you to stop what you're doing and provide a response. If you create a Notebook containing nothing but copies of your listings, no matter where you are or what you're doing you're just a moment away from answering that random question from a potential buyer or buyer's agent.

7. Manage Buyers
Populate your buyer Notebooks with Notes exactly as you would with paper files. Here are some things you can include:

From the Vault: Real Estate Confronts Reality (1997)

"Real estate professionals will have to transform themselves into online transactional experts, offering high-touch data-driven consultative advice, while still resolving the personal and emotional complexities involved in buying a home."

- Notes from initial buyer consultation.
- Client's "wish list."
- Copy of buyer's pre-approval letter.
- PDF copies of listings sent to the buyer.
- PDF copies of home tours and showings.
- Audio notes taken while on home tours.
- Photos taken while on home tours.
- Copies of disclosures relating to homes for which your buyer has a potential interest.
- Copies of CMAs prepared on homes for which your buyer has a potential interest.
- Copies of contracts prepared on behalf of your buyers.
- Copies of addenda created on behalf of your buyers.
- Copies of inspection reports.
- Copies of radon reports.
- Copies of closing documents.

8. Store Contract Info
Real estate is practiced very differently depending upon where you are in the country. In some states agents use standard contracts and never modify those contracts, in other states they often create contracts and frequently modify, tailor or otherwise customize them for each unique client situation. If you work in a market where contract preparation is part of your job description, we recommend that you create a notebook called "Contract Stuff." Include in it all of the various language and provisions that you consistently use. This will save you time each and every time you need to prepare a contract for a client.

9. Share with Clients
In total, Evernote offers four unique ways to share a Note from within a Note: email, Twitter, Facebook or through a uniquely created URL within Evernote. The two methods you'll use most often with clients are email and URL.

The email option is simple and works just like you'd expect: simply email the exact contents of a Note to an email recipient. The URL option is one of Evernote's coolest features. When you choose this option a unique URL is created on Evernote.com, the end result of which is a publicly viewable "mini-website" displaying the contents of the applicable Note.

Another function allows for the sharing of an entire Notebook. Depending on the level of subscription you have, a shared Notebook may be only viewed (basic) or viewed, modified and re-shared (premium).

10. Use Audio Notes
When you're not able to use a keyboard, you can create new Notes (or annotate existing Notes) using Evernote's audio Note functionality. To create an audio Note you simply press the microphone icon (located on the primary menu at the top of every Note) and start speaking. When you're finished, press the red "Done" button and an audio file will appear inside your Note. It's that easy.

You can then press "Play" inside the embedded audio file to listen to what you recorded. Don't like it? Just delete it by backspacing over it or by selecting it and clicking the "delete" key and start recording a new audio Note.

Adding explanatory audio comments within an existing Note is a great feature, particularly given how often you send documents to clients that require some level of explanation. This can be a significant timesaver and service-perception-enhancer. Using this approach provides a more personal and human connection with your clients, and your voice inflection and tone provides a more nuanced level of communication.

11. Remember Everything

Due to the sheer volume of documents involved in the typical real estate transaction you often misplace or misfile those documents. In addition, you frequently need to

transform a past client into a referral-providing-raving-fan. Conversely, when you can't do that, it can have the opposite effect. Evernote is the perfect solution for these common challenges.

That said, we recommend that you get into the habit of saving every document of significance into

To leverage Evernote to its full potential from an organizational perspective, we also recommend that you get in the habit of using tags in all of your Notes. Over time, as you consistently use tags, it will make your archived material even more valuable and easier to locate.

> ## Over time, you will enjoy substantial gains in productivity and efficiency as you perfect the population and composition of Evernote templates. You'll never have to reinvent the wheel again.

find important documents quickly, i.e., a set of closing documents for a client needing that information for their attorney or CPA.

Few activities can make you look more organized and professional than when you can react instantly to such requests and provide exactly what was asked for in a matter of a moment or two. These are the actions that can

Evernote; for starters, scan every set of closing documents. A great way to do this is to purchase an external scanner that can be configured to do exactly that. Along these lines, we suggest the Fujitsu ScanSnap as a good option, which is available in a variety of models for both Windows and Mac.

12. Using Handwritten Notes

If you have an iPad—and if you don't, we suggest that you reconsider that position—there are some great "hand written note" apps on the market. Our favorite, after trying them all, is NoteShelf; available on iTunes for $5.99. This app is very functional, beautifully designed, easy-to-use and allows you to upload Notes directly into Evernote.

SOURCE EVERNOTE

Resources for Agents

- Various Video Courses on vdemy.com
- Webinars (Evernote 101 and Evernote 102) on CoffeewithKrisstina.com.
- Video Tutorials on Frugyl.com

Evernote Web Clipper

From interests to research, save anything you see online—including text, links and images—into your Evernote account with a single click.

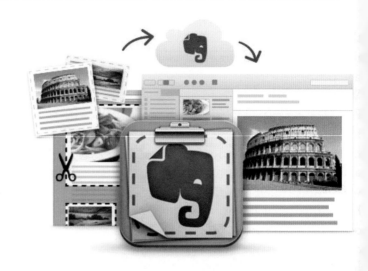

[Get Web Clipper for Chrome] For other browsers

 Works with Evernote Business

Research made easy
With one click, clip part or all of any webpage, including text, images, and links.

Save your interests
Collect everything that inspires you online. Have it forever, even if the original goes away.

Read anywhere
In a rush? Clip webpages to Evernote and read them later on any device you use.

SOURCE EVERNOTE

If you like taking handwritten notes this is a great way to have the "best of both worlds," being able to write manually and still upload directly into the digital realm. The combination of NoteShelf and Evernote allows you to go almost completely paperless from a note taking perspective.

OTHER USEFUL FUNCTIONALITIES

1. Web Clipper

Another important tool is the "Web Clipper" browser plugin (see below), which creates Notes out of entire webpages, excerpts of webpages or simply the URL of a webpage, depending upon which of the "clipping options" you elect to use. This is a great way to save and bookmark things you find on the web you want to come back to later. It also effectively makes your bookmarks accessible from any device. This is among the most valuable of the functionalities we've found within Evernote.

As one of your first acts we recommend that you download the Web Clipper into the browser(s) of your choice and start using it immediately. Once you have it installed, when you're on a page you want to clip, you simply click on the "Clip to Evernote" button, which will now be a fixed item on your browser toolbar, and a window pops open. You can then add a title, tags, notes, select which Notebook to place the Note in and elect whether to clip the entire page, a specific excerpt from the page (highlight the portion of the page you want to clip before you click on the "Clip to Evernote" icon) or just the URL. You then click "Save" and a new Note is automatically created.

2. Evernote Email Address

Another valuable functionality is

the capability of e-mailing directly into Evernote and having that email automatically create a unique Note. When you sign-up you are given an Evernote e-mail address specifically for this purpose. Once you add that Evernote e-mail address into your address book (so that it auto populates when you're drafting an e-mail), it becomes a very easy matter to e-mail directly into Evernote. Here is a list of things that we routinely e-mail into Evernote:

- E-mails we want to be sure we reply to later.

- Things we want to read later.

- Important Google voice messages we may receive via e-mail.

- Important items we discover on Zite (zite.com).

- Important e-mails from clients.

- Anything that we don't want to get lost in the crush in most people's e-mail inboxes these days.

Not only that, but you can also email items directly into specific Notebooks you've created by simply adding "@" and then the exact name of the Notebook you want the email to be placed into once it has been created in the subject line of your email.

3. Drag and Drop

Another Evernote feature we love almost as much as the Web Clipper is its drag and drop functionality. With this technology you can literally drag and drop just about anything onto the Evernote icon on your computer desktop and it will automatically create a Note.

Looking at the image (Mac desktop) you can see the Evernote icon in the lower right corner. You can simply drag a file down onto the icon and a new, unique Note will be automatically created. This is a great technique for creating Notes from random files, highlighted paragraphs from text documents, etc. The two most common ways we've found for creating Notes are by the Web Clipper and dragging and dropping.

4. Use as a Teleprompter

One of the most important things we do as real estate professionals is present information to others. The degree to which we're successful often hinges on our ability to speak off the cuff, contemporaneously and with authority. This is of particular significance when competing for business in a listing presentation. The iPad and Evernote create a wonderful combination and solution. Prepare a "bullet list" agenda within Evernote for a situation where you're going to be speaking and use your iPad as a pseudo teleprompter.

5. Mobile Scan

There are a number of mobile apps available on the market that have the ability to send information directly into Evernote. There are two that we have used which work well for this purpose, JotNot Pro ($1.99) and Genius Scan (free). Both are available on Apple's App Store. With either of these apps, you can "scan" (basically, take a photo) anything and send it directly into Evernote. This is a great way to save something you might have written on a whiteboard or a small document of some variety. Be aware that while you can scan multipage documents with either of these apps, we don't recommend it, as scanning multiple pages tends to be a nuisance. However, in a pinch, having the ability to scan a document from anywhere using one of these apps can be a huge benefit.

6. Content Creation Machine

Think of Evernote as the place to load your "content creation machine" with raw material. Here are a few ideas:

- Create a Notebook called "Hyperlocal."

- Create a Notebook called "Blog post ideas."

- Create a Notebook called "To be posted on Facebook."

- Create a Notebook called "For my real estate clients."

Drag and Drop

SOURCE EVERNOTE

Dropbox and Evernote Comparison

- **Setup:** Cloud-based.

- **Platform:** Multiple platforms.

- **Sync:** Can create folder on desktop which syncs with cloud.

- **Free Version:** up to 2GB total storage.

- **Emphasis:** Storage/temporary storage.
    FILES. LARGE files.
    Sharing.
    Backing files up.

- **File Size:** Limit to 300MB via Website

- **Creative Element:** None.

- **Comments:** Think of it as a backup hard drive with great
    sharing functionality.

- **Setup:** Cloud-based.

- **Platform:** Multiple platforms.

- **Sync:** Desktop version also available which syncs with cloud.

- **Free Version:** up to 50MB/month.

- **Emphasis:** Permanent storage.
    NOTES (which can contain certain types of file).
    Notebooks (collections of notes).
    Sharing of Notes and Notebooks.

- **File Size:** Limited to 50MB (so not great for large file storage).

- **Creative Element:** Note taking.
    Web-clipping.
    Drag & drop into Notes.
    Audio Notes.
    Tagging.
    Emailing into Notes.

- **Comments:** Keyword, tag and OCR searchable.
    Can scan directly into Evernote.
    Think of it as the center of your digital universe
    for most everything EXCEPT large files.

SOURCE REALSURE, INC

- Create a Notebook called "To be tweeted."

Once you get in the habit of populating these "aggregation silos," you'll always have a ready supply of content on hand for whatever you need (blogs, videos, tweets, Facebook posts, etc.).

And if you're a blogger, you know what that experience is like (at least for most): you have five, 10 or maybe even 100 ideas in process for every post you actually finish. Evernote can be used as the perfect "blog incubator" in the sense that you can access your "in process" posts from anywhere, whenever inspiration strikes. We've edited blog posts from restaurants, grocery store lines and while sitting in our car in the middle of a parking lot. Having the ability to do this is truly invaluable. Here is the process we recommend for incubating blog posts in Evernote:

- Create two Notebooks for blogging: one for posts in process and the other for posts that have been published.

- Create a new Note inside the "work in process" Notebook whenever a new idea strikes.

- Create an outline or an overview of the post.

- Start filling the post as you're able.

- Tweak, tweak and tweak some more.

- Once the post is ready for publishing, transfer it to WordPress.

- Complete the post in WordPress.

- Move the Note from "blogs in process" to "blogs published."

In the final analysis, the blog post "lives" inside Evernote far longer than it does inside WordPress. We find the context of Evernote to be more conducive to editing than the context of WordPress, primarily because it's just so much easier to access Evernote than WordPress from a mobile device.

COMPARISON TO DROPBOX

A question that comes up frequently when discussing Evernote is this: "I'm already using Dropbox; isn't that the same as Evernote?" We have created a summary that is reflected in the comparison table.

SUMMARY

It may take you several attempts to get the hang of Evernote. This is a common experience that we've heard from a number of Evernote's most fervent supporters. So if you try and it doesn't grab you at first, keep this in mind before giving up on this "electronic Swiss Army knife." It can become the hub of your digital world, as it has for nearly 50 million people already. We consider Evernote to be one of the most versatile and powerful organizational tools in existence, and we encourage you to make it a priority to learn how to "remember everything." We think you'll be glad you did!

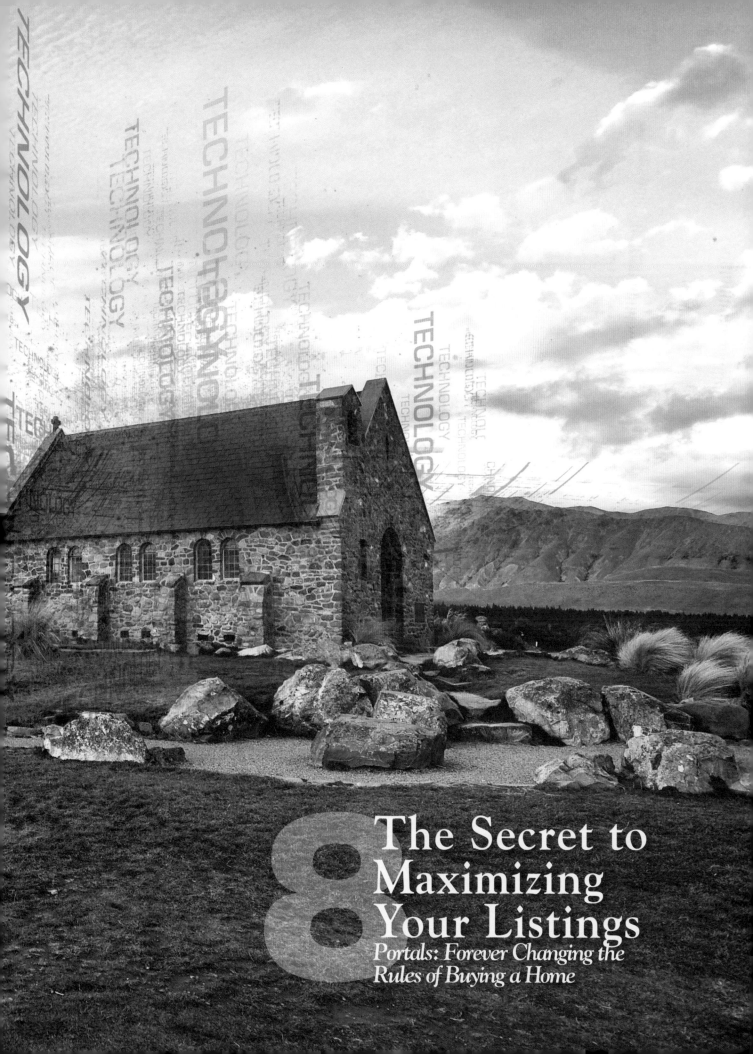

The Secret to Maximizing Your Listings

8

Portals: Forever Changing the Rules of Buying a Home

The Secret to Maximizing Your Listings

The once vulnerable consumer—who for decades has been beholden to the traditional real estate machine for almost all types of real estate information for which brokers and agents have served as gatekeepers—through the evolution of the Internet, has now been given unprecedented access to that same data. This has transformed homebuyers into an autonomous, information hungry, mega-force in the marketplace. And their rapidly expanding and evolving expectations and demands are setting new standards for how homes are being bought today and how they are going to be bought and sold in the future.

The fundamentals that allowed outside third-party players to enter real estate, aggregate real estate information and make this data available through a variety of portals didn't happen overnight, nor was it a surprise. This has been in the making for approximately 15 years and has been analyzed many times. "If you want to see where the first warning signs for the real estate brokerage to begin to prepare for this pending shift start, read the 1997 book, *Real Estate Confronts Reality* by Tom Dooley, Stefan Swanepoel and Michael Abelson. Most recently we drew your attention to the importance of this subject matter in the 2012 *Swanepoel TRENDS Report*. It can be downloaded for free at RETrends.com (see Chapter 3 - *The Internet. Data Lines will be Drawn; Will IPOs Create Champions*).

But alas, the real estate brokerage industry was overconfident and too stubborn to move from its comfort zone and change a business model that many thought was (and which many think still is) working fine. Being conceited is one of the largest errors any person, company or industry can make. In business, arrogance usually opens the door for "outsiders" to enter and seize the "innovation opportunity."

It wasn't that long ago that when consumers wondered about the value of their home they had to hire a licensed appraiser to do the math. And if they wanted information about a listing down the street, they called a real estate agent who had exclusive access to the pool of "homes for sale" within that area's MLS. That was the way the world worked before aggregators and real estate portals.

Enter a new group of companies to which the industry gave arguably its most valuable asset—that body of real estate information—and within approximately a decade many of the rules and norms that had previously dominated the industry were almost completely redefined. By providing larger accessibility to home buying and selling information, and higher levels of customer services, new companies such as Zillow, Trulia, Realtor.com, Yahoo Real Estate, Homes.com and others gained widespread popularity fairly quickly.

Aggregators, websites and portals that were ridiculed, ignored or belittled a short decade ago are today as much an integral part of the real estate industry as the brokerages, companies and agents that have until recently enjoyed exclusivity to that precious data. Increasingly we're noticing that in many regards these new players are actually setting the tone and the direction by which we believe a lot of future decisions in the brokerage space will be measured. We have researched many of these companies, spoken to their leadership and learned about their structures, the services they offer and generally how they go about doing what they do. And we're impressed. In residential real estate these companies are rapidly becoming the standard.

In almost every survey undertaken by anyone, including NAR, the California Association of REALTORS® (CAR), etc., they virtually all report that 98 percent of all home searches take place on the Internet. Clearly it has become the industry norm for buying a home—as

transaction, read Chapters 9 and 10 of this Report respectively).

REAL ESTATE PORTALS

According to data from Experian Marketing Services (experian.com), the top five listing portals— Zillow, Trulia, Realtor.com, Yahoo Real Estate and Homes.com—continue to grow their combined market share (see charts on Pages 116 and 117, respectively). In January 2013 the top 10 real estate websites had a total market share of 42 percent with the top five garnering almost 80 percent of that traffic (these figures do not include mobile visits that will increase the market share of the top five even further).

The consumers' hunger for real estate data isn't abating and, in fact,

- Own vs. rent ratio.
- Ethnicity demographics.
- Average household's age.
- Average household's income.
- Average rent.
- Percentage of college graduates.
- Unemployment rate.
- Public Assistance.
- Percent tax assessment.
- Distance from work.
- Sex offenders.

Put this all together and it's clear that portals are impacting the home search process and, by extension, the MLSs,

> **In almost every survey undertaken by anyone, including the National Association of REALTORS® (NAR), the California Association of REALTORS® (CAR), etc. virtually all report that some 98% of all home searches take place on the Internet.**

it has for most other purchases and activities. None of this should come as a surprise to anyone.

Today, real estate information is readily available online and people have access to information, anywhere, anytime. Four out of every five people on the planet own a mobile phone and more than 50 percent of those phones have browser capabilities (for more details on the mobile revolution and the paperless

the government has even gotten involved to satisfy the public's increased demand for this kind of information. CensusConnect Realty (census-connect.com), a software development company, has taken advantage of a U.S. Census Bureau API (api.census.gov) that provides access to 2010 Census data and developed a browser plug-in that adds "block level" census data to aggregators, portals and others such as:

brokers and listing agents. In the days ahead we're going to see more and more technological innovation from these companies as they all vie for the homebuyers' attention and compete to be first in line to fulfill their desires in the home search space.

DATA ACCURACY

Data accuracy is a hot button issue in any conversation regarding portals. Many agents boycott portals for this very reason and there have been numerous comments from brokers and agents of outdated or incorrect data appearing on Zillow, Trulia, etc.

Brokers and MLSs can control where their listings are being syndicated and used on websites and portals but many fail to do so effectively due to the perceived volume of work involved. From an MLS perspective the issues are compounded by the varying terms of use involved with each syndicator. However, it's important to note that portals are for the most part (the exception being when they allow their subscribers to edit data directly on the portals' sites) merely conduits or "pipelines" that channel information provided by broker sites or intermediary sites like ListHub (listhub.com) and Point2NLS (point2.com). Data accuracy is clearly a problem, and a complex one to resolve.

PORTAL PRODUCT OFFERINGS FOR AGENTS

There are a whole host of products and services offered to agents by the larger portals, and an entire book could be written on this subject alone. It's important to note up front that there are in certain cases a variety of "big picture" factors that determine what services are available to a given agent, including decisions "upstream" from the agent at the broker, brokerage and even the brand or franchise level. So, the first thing any agent needs to do is understand how those decisions impact or limit what they can or cannot do.

Conceptually, the leading portals offer similar listing management and lead generation products, but there are various distinctions that make each unique so have each company give you a detailed overview of their latest products and services so that you can understand the differences. Here is a brief overview of the larger and more popular services offered by the portals at the time of going to print:.

Top Five Real Estate Websites Ranked by % Market Share

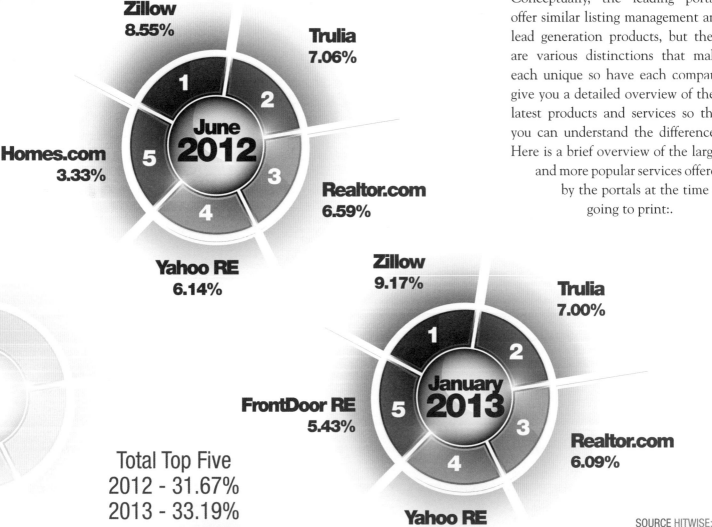

Zillow 8.55%

Trulia 7.06%

Homes.com 3.33%

June 2012

Realtor.com 6.59%

Yahoo RE 6.14%

Zillow 9.17%

Trulia 7.00%

FrontDoor RE 5.43%

January 2013

Realtor.com 6.09%

Yahoo RE 5.50%

Total Top Five
2012 - 31.67%
2013 - 33.19%

SOURCE HITWISE;
EXPERIAN MARKETING SERVICES

Today's consumers are far more knowledgeable and empowered than they were just a short decade ago.

1. Zillow

Zillow allows real estate agents to provide their listings to Zillow and offers lead generation tools and services. The costs of the services range from free to variable, based on the ZIP code (details at bit.ly/14rvdeT). Here are some things to consider:

- When you send your listings to Zillow, you can "protect" them by paying to ensure that no other agent's photo or contact information appears next to your listing. This is what agents are paying for when they buy Zillow's lead generation service: effectively, the ability to generate leads by appearing in searches done within zip codes on listings that are not "protected" by the applicable listing agents.

- While you can ensure that your photo appears next to your listings by simply completing a free agent profile on Zillow, this will not block other agent photos and contact information from appearing below your photo.

- Whatever you pay for on Zillow extends to Zillow.com, Zillow Mobile, Yahoo! Homes, Google Now and HGTV Frontdoor. Even if you decide not to use Zillow's services, you should absolutely complete your profile. It's free for listing agents to create a profile, complete with contact information, photo, reviews and external links.

2. Trulia

Trulia's packages are conceptually similar to Zillow's, but with some differences. Here is a summary of Trulia's offerings:

- Trulia's primary agent and brokerage offering is called Trulia Pro (Plus, Deluxe and Elite). The plans are priced according the number of listings an agent has at any one time and ranges from $39/month for three featured listings, to $99/month for 10 and $199/month for 20-featured listings. Each packages some variations of features, the most important of which is the "ad-free featured listings" which is only available with the Elite package.

- Featured listings are the default presentation for a ZIP code or city search and featured listings have the agent contact info highlighted in the light blue bar. Note that there can be a "Featured Ad" from another agent next to the listing when another agent has purchased ZIP code or city advertising. ZIP code and city advertising is charged as a percentage of the number of impressions that area gets per month. Contracts are sold in blocks of 20 percent of the total number of impressions and in 3-month increments.

- Trulia displays up to 15 listings on each search results page and there is usually a display box showing four local agents at the bottom of that Web page. This is what is called "appearing in the rotation." The number of times and places that a Trulia Pro agent appears in this ad is dependent on whether that agent bought advertising as well as the level of the subscription. Some brokerages have purchased "protection" for their listings and in those cases they secure the right side "Contact Agent" space and the block ad that usually has the other agents listed on the page.

3. Realtor.com

Realtor.com has several product offerings, including Showcase Listing Enhancement and Market Snapshot. Showcase Listing Enhancement does several things, including giving an agent's listings preferential positioning in search results made on Realtor.com, and which also allows the agent to:

- Upload videos.

- Manage and add photos.

- Edit text descriptions; up to 2,500 characters, which are a lot more than allowed in typical MLS descriptions.

- Add a headline.

- Use a "Special Message Box" to highlight a unique aspect of the property.

- Promote open houses.

Market Snapshot provides "local information delivered at the neighborhood level." It "provides a method to keep consumers updated on activities in their immediate neighborhood, gives regular reports

and graphics on what has come on the market and how long it takes neighborhood homes to sell and uses statistics on changes in asking to list price, indicating a potential buyer's or seller's market."

Best Practices

There is a lot of misunderstanding surrounding the aggregators and portals, and there is so much for an agent to know to make the best decisions says, Leslie Ebersole of Chicago's Baird & Warner.

1. Agents need to understand their brokerage company or their franchise/brand strategy with respect to syndication, as these "corporate" decisions taken "upstream" from the agent can affect what the agent can and cannot do.

2. Understanding how these

programs work and what you're going to get for your dollar is critically important. Many agents, who attempt some of these services, when they don't get the results they wanted, blame the system, when the problem really lies in the agent's understanding of how the programs actually works.

3. When you buy ZIP codes you cross over from pure listing management to lead generation. This is neither right nor wrong, it's just important that you understand the shift. Usually by having a "layered presence" on multiple portals (meaning a combination of ad spend, listing syndication and agent reviews) you get to the point where the payoff can be sizeable.

Unique Users - December 2012

22.0 million — Zillow

11.6 million — Trulia

10.7 million — Move Inc (Includes Realtor.com)

SOURCE COMSCORE

CASE STUDY

To better understand the inner workings of a portal we selected the largest portal, Zillow, for our case study.

ZILLOW

1. Background

As with many products and services, the concept came from real-world challenges when company founders had endured similar difficulties when purchasing their own homes. These experienced technology executives were frustrated by the dearth of real estate information available on the Internet. They didn't understand why they should they have to scour public records or call real estate agents to get the information they needed. If they called too late in the day, as an example of one common frustration, they'd simply have to wait until the next day to get answers if their real estate agent didn't reply quickly.

These were problems that needed to be fixed and they set out to do just that by building a comprehensive online source for real estate data that would arm consumers with the information and tools they needed to make informed decisions about homes, real estate and mortgages.

They hoped their new website would attract a million visitors in its first month. That goal was surpassed in three days, indicating a very smart marketing launch but also validating that easy access to information about homes was in even higher demand than most people anticipated. Although a wakeup call for certain, few could have predicted the magnitude of change or the speed with which it would take place.

2. Zestimates

In the beginning, Zillow did not carry for-sale home listings, but merely Zillow's estimations of home valuations—ingeniously called "Zestimates." The Zillow team always hoped to include real estate listings on the site but regulatory and business challenges rose up along the way, most specifically in the form of rules concerning access to MLS listings. Because of limits placed on the use of those listings, the Company was forced to get creative and Zestimates was born and soon struck a chord with consumers.

The database upon which these calculations were made included information gathered from public sources regarding a home's location, size and prior sale price. Many inside the real estate industry have criticized the overall accuracy of Zestimates. According to Zillow the national mean variance in their Zestimates is 8.7 percent. Whether you think that is significant or not, it appears that this inconsistency has had little impact on the popularity of this estimation tool with homeowners.

3. Listings

In December 2006, nearly a year after its initial launch, Zillow began accepting listings from brokers and homeowners themselves. The site's listing inventory exploded, and within 90 days more than 50,000 for-sale homes were listed on Zillow. And by the end of 2007 the website had a half-million for-sale listings, plus an additional 36,000 FSBO and 133,000 Make Me Move® homes (i.e.,

homes that were not officially on the market, but for which owners named a "dream price" at which point they would potentially sell their home).

Savvy agents and brokers quickly saw the tremendous buzz that Zillow was generating and recognized the marketing opportunity borne of the Internet traffic alone. They wanted to have their listings seen by those browsing the Company's website looking for information about cities and neighborhoods; a site visited by millions of people who were about to become home shoppers.

During this version, an agent who wanted their listing on the site had to manually reenter the MLS listing on Zillow and then Zillow included the listing—complete with the agent's name—in its searchable database. Interested buyers had a means of contacting the agent and the agent got a free lead.

4. Advertising

Along the way, Zillow began to accept ads from agents who wanted their names, photos and contact information made accessible to those searching for homes in their areas. They also began to accept listings from data feed providers who had permission from an MLS to redistribute syndicated listings. So, seven years after being founded, Zillow's website and mobile applications now enjoy over 45 million unique users per month—a number that dwarfs all previous comparable statistics in the history of the real estate brokerage business. Whether it's the Internet, mobile or Zillow—the rules have changed for buying and selling a home.

In February 2011 Zillow and Yahoo launched an exclusive partnership that brought together two sites to create the largest real estate network on the web, thereby allowing Zillow to become Yahoo! Real Estate's exclusive provider of for-sale listings and its real estate advertising sales force.

5. Acquisitions

In earlier editions of the *Swanepoel TRENDS Report* we advised that successful IPOs (Initial Public Offering) usually generate significant cash for companies, and we predicted that Zillow's IPO would lead them to outplay most of their competition by rolling up and acquiring the necessary assets to become the dominant player in the industry.

Well they've definitely started doing exactly that. In November 2011 Zillow announced its acquisition of Diverse Solutions (diversesolutions. com), which provides listing content and property search functionality. In May 2012 they acquired RentJuice (rentjuice.com), a company that offers tools to property management companies. The acquisition helped springboard Zillow into Zillow Rentals in October 2012, a marketplace and suite of tools for rental professionals.

In October 2012 Zillow purchased Buyfolio (buyfolio.com), which provides agent and buyer tools that make online shopping for a home easier and more organized. The site gives homebuyers a simple, real-time snapshot of their home search, and allows the buyer's agent to add local knowledge, notes and additional listings. Either party can drop properties into "the folio" or comment on other properties that were also added. Coordinated showings of the properties can result, and each property can be flagged for follow-up or elimination from consideration.

In November of the same year, Zillow acquired the map-based rental and real estate website HotPads (hotpads. com). In the same month they also acquired Mortech (mortech.com), a 25-year-old software and services company that provides mortgage-related solutions to lenders, bankers and credit unions. It was Zillow's first acquisition in the mortgage arena and enabled them to offer promotion and productivity tools to professionals in the mortgage industry. These tools will aid mortgage professionals in business management and the conversion of prospective borrowers into actual borrowers. This latest acquisition augments the growth of the company's loan market, Zillow

Mortgage Marketplace, which in 2012 received nearly 12 million loan requests.

6. The Business Model

From home valuations to information about financing to online listings, the information available on Zillow's website has always been free to consumers. The company's principal source of income is the Premier Agent Program, which accounts for more than 70 percent of its revenues, with Zillow Mortgage Marketplace and institutional advertising accounting for the remainder.

Zillow hoped to attract a million visitors in its first month. That goal was surpassed in three days.

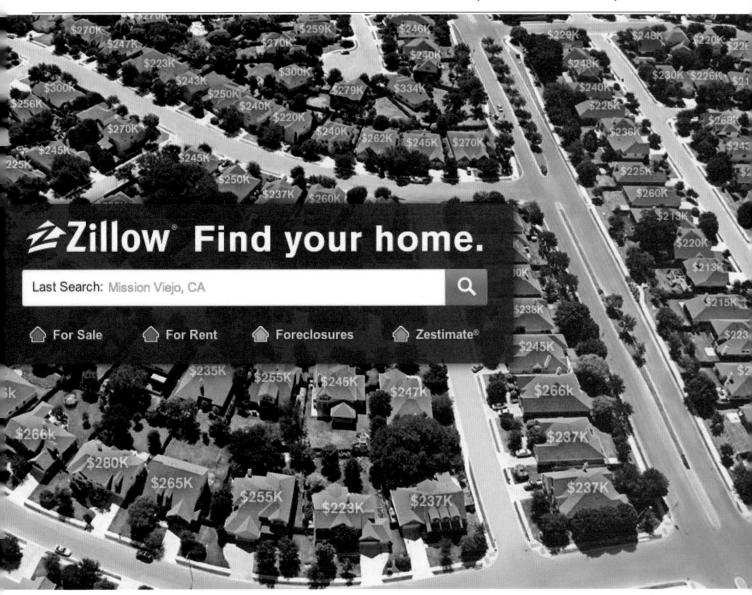

Zillow recognized that revenue potential from agent advertising was not unlimited, so in its quest for new revenue streams, the Company recognized the importance of providing value to its current clients while trying to acquire new ones. To that end they created a package of tools they could provide for free, or at a very low cost that would enhance the value agents find in the platform, thus increasing loyalty and retention rates.

For example, agents who paid at least $10 per month (the cost of the "premier silver" tier of services) received Customer Relationship Management (CRM) tools to help track and prioritize requests from customers. In summer 2012 the company added free customized websites for its Premier Agents and offered non-premier agents the same site for $10 per month. It's expected they will do the same with Buyfolio, rolling it into the Premier Agent Program as an added value at no charge, but offering it to non-advertising agents for a nominal fee.

Their strategy here is to have many hundreds of thousands of agents using their suite of—mostly free—productivity tools. And then to have a smaller portion actually paying for services in sort of a freemium model (software where the base product/ service is offered free of charge but payment is required for the advance features). The strategy is all about shifting from a seller of advertising, which is very finite and sort of monolithic, to a provider of a SaaS-based (Software As A Service, also known as "on-demand software" that is centrally hosted on the cloud) suite of productivity tools of which ads, or

From the Vault: Real Estate Confronts Reality (1997)

"Forget the listing race to get to one million listings. Think of a new world, with instant access to one 100 million homes in the U.S."

lead gen, is a part. At Q4 2012 Zillow had 30,000 subscribers (up from 15,000 a year prior) as compared to Trulia that had 23,000 subscribers (up from 17,000 the year prior). Realtor.com doesn't charge agents a subscription for enhancing listings so there is no comparable number to share here.

7. Consumer Traffic

So, what is causing consumers to go to the Zillow site before they go to yours—that's if they're even aware of your site? Here are a few of the key drivers:

- More comprehensive data including multiple outside databases (like Walk Scores and school rankings) as well as proprietary databases Zillow has developed that no other site has.

- The largest inventory of properties from multiple sources: for sale, pre-market (foreclosures, pre-foreclosures), builder, for sale by owner, Make Me Move® homes as well as rentals. Their inventory is not limited to just what agents put into the MLS because Zillow's visitors want to see a picture of the entire market.

- Opportunity to interact with the site—consumers and agents can input or correct home facts which may affect the Zestimate. Owners can comment on the property, citing what they think are unique features that would make it more valuable. Buying partners can compare notes with their agent and weed through properties before ever visiting a home.

- Saved searches with update email notifications, open house alerts and property reports on homes.

8. The Future for Zillow

Zillow has been quite candid about its plans for the future. In its most recent 10-K filing for the fiscal year ending December 2012 they stated the following about their growth strategies:

- **Focus on Consumers.** Maintain our unwavering focus on consumers and leverage our industry independence to enhance existing products and services and develop new offerings with broad consumer appeal.

- **Enhance Our Living Database.** Enhance the information in our database of homes, and use it as the foundation for new analyses, insights and tools to inform consumers throughout the home ownership lifecycle.

- **Leverage Our Mobile Leadership.** Innovate and expand our offerings for mobile devices, launching more applications and extending our brand and products across additional mobile platforms.

- **Deepen, Strengthen and Expand Our Marketplaces.** Deepen and strengthen our marketplaces by creating new opportunities for high-quality consumer-initiated connections with real estate, rental, mortgage and home improvement professionals when consumers want their services. Our living database of homes provides a foundation on which we can build new consumer and professional marketplaces in other home-related categories.

- **Efficiently Increase Brand Awareness.** Expand public relations, Social Media, content distribution and advertising programs to efficiently increase brand awareness.

- **Expand Our Platform.** Expand our platform beyond advertising services for real estate, rental, mortgage and home improvement professionals by developing additional marketing and business technology solutions to help those professionals manage and grow their businesses and personal brands.

- **Optimize Opportunities for Premier Agent Participation.** Optimize opportunities for Premier Agent participation in our marketplaces

through development of a broad variety of marketing and business technology solutions.

- **Leverage Our Sales Force.** Leverage our sales force's expertise with new advertising and technology offerings.

- **Pursue Strategic Opportunities.** Pursue strategic opportunities, including commercial relationships and acquisitions, to strengthen our market position, enhance our capabilities and accelerate our growth.

9. Partnering With Google

In 2012 Zillow announced that it had teamed with Google to bring

real estate search to Google Now. According to Brian Boero of 1000 Watt Consulting (1000watt.net), "It proactively grabs or alerts you to things in categories like travel, sports, traffic, events, places and package delivery. Information is presented via "cards" that appear when you want them to." Google describes it this way: Google Now gets you just the right information at just the right time. It tells you today's weather before you start your day, how much traffic to expect before you leave for work, when the next train will arrive as you're standing on the platform, or your favorite team's score while they're playing. And the best part? All of this happens automatically. Cards appear throughout the day at the moment you need them.

Google Now gets you just the right information at just the right time.

It tells you today's weather before you start your day, how much traffic to expect before you leave for work, when the next train will arrive as you're standing on the platform, or your favorite team's score while they're playing.

And the best part? All of this happens automatically. Cards appear throughout the day at the moment you need them.

Boero also noted that, "Looking inward to the industry, I think this scrambles the 'syndication' narrative a bit. For years, brokers have thought about this as sending their listings to websites that compete with their own website; or sending their listings to mobile apps that compete with their own app or apps. I also think, paradoxically, that as Zillow, Trulia and Realtor.com take brokers to places to which they would not otherwise be able to go, those brokers increase their leverage. While brokers need to reach consumers in new places, the online players absolutely must do so. As the listings pipeline extends into new territory there is more of it to sabotage."

SUMMARY

In *Real Estate Confronts Reality* four chapters were dedicated to the consumer and to technology. We're not going to restate the many predictions made 15 years ago, but we would like to mention one paragraph from *Chapter 9: Is Tech the Ticket to Ride?* that stood out upon reading the book again the other day. "Changes are occurring with ever-increasing speed, and the effect on the real estate industry will be enormous. The impact that technology can and will have is also no longer limited to improving the existing operations but in fundamentally changing the total structure of an industry." Remember this was written in 1997.

By 2013 these words have become a reality on so many different levels.

More specifically, we can state that portals and aggregators exist and are successful today because they fill a void that the existing players in the industry didn't care enough about, deem important enough to fill or didn't move fast enough to address in a meaningful way. We, as an industry, resisted as we have done so many times in the past. When will we learn? Change is a constant. Change happens to all of us, continuously, and innovation is healthy.

Remember: The consumer is always in the driver's seat.

The founders of Trulia (Sami Inkinen and Pete Flint) and Zillow (Rich Barton and Lloyd Frink) are of course also consumers, and were also home buying consumers. They were frustrated at the level and nature of the service that the real estate industry in general was—or was not—delivering. They couldn't understand why they were not able to have access to usable real estate information, how they wanted it and when they wanted it. The fact that brokers and agents wanted consumers to call them to get anything beyond the most cursory of information was not acceptable. So they set out to change that. And they did.

Today's consumers are far more knowledgeable and empowered than they were back in the mid 90s, just a short decade ago. Remember 15 years ago a significant number of homebuyers were still Baby Boomers! And they weren't at the leading edge of the technological revolution, which had so clearly begun to take place. So, brokers and agents touted that the predictions of imminent change were overrated.

And then a new generation grew a decade or more older and Gen-X and -Y started to manage their own home search process. En masse they demanded more transparency and more access to real estate information. As a result, the industry felt the power of the consumer voice, first asking for more info, and secondly asking for a new way to do business.

In the final analysis, the home search process has changed: it has become faster, more efficient and self-contained. The Internet and mobile technology have aided in opening up a new doorway to the consumer. Aggregators and portals like Zillow, Trulia, Homes.com and Move, Inc. have seized the opportunity and are reaching the consumer in the very early stages of the home search process. All three companies are public, are well capitalized and are set for potentially significant growth. The smart move is to use these portals and aggregators to reach out to more prospects and clients and take your existing service practices to the next level by offering a more efficient and effective service.

Online real estate portals are today an integral and important part of the home buyer-agent relationship, and their influence and impact are expected to grow significantly in the years to come.

NETWORK SEARCH

9 Anytime, Anyplace, Anywhere

MOBILE: *The Most Significant Invention of Our Time*

Anytime, Anyplace, Anywhere

Mobile is an abbreviated way of saying "mobile computing," or the use of computers and communication devices in a "transportable" fashion. The first hand-held mobile phone dates back to 1973. Initially growth was very slow and after some 20 years there were only 12.4 million mobile users worldwide. But in the following 22 years the number of mobile users exploded to more than 6 billion, vaulting mobile phones to the most popular and widely used technology of all time. For the first time in human history, about four out of every five people on the planet own a similar device and are connected to each other like never before.

"Game changer" is one of the most oft-used and misused expressions of our day. Rarely does it truly apply. However, it's no stretch to call the Smartphone a legitimate game changer. Evolving into much more than just a phone, it has become the holy grail of devices into which has been incorporated all of the technological developments of the last three decades in a single, portable, relatively inexpensive device that everyone will have—sorry, already has. Mobile is quite likely the most significant device and tool to be introduced during our lifetime.

CELLPHONES AND SMARTPHONES
The race for dominance in the mobile world is most certainly a trillion dollar battle.

In 2012 Samsung, a South Korean company, overtook longtime leader Nokia to become the #1 player in mobile phones with a 29 percent worldwide market share according to Fortune magazine (fortune.com). In the Smartphone category, Samsung is also #1 worldwide, while in the U.S. most analysts put them at a tie with Apple at a 33 percent market share. Phone companies are so eager to stock Samsung phones that they've all abandoned their practice of requesting exclusivity. Last summer AT&T, Sprint, T-Mobile and Verizon all launched the Samsung Galaxy S lll simultaneously.

With regard to operating platform it's also down to a two horse race. Once dominated by Research in Motion (RIM; blackberry.com), Samsung's relationship with Google (maker of the Android operating system) has helped to propel Droid to the #1 spot. Google's Android phones and Apple's iPhone now control 89 percent of the market according to comScore (comscore.com). This is up significantly as these two players accounted for 51 percent just two years ago. Meanwhile RIM, who has seen its market share drop from 34 percent two years ago to just seven percent at the end of 2012, is most likely going to lose their number three slot to Microsoft. No one else really matters.

Meanwhile the Apple vs. Samsung legal battle over trademark infringement may just turn out to be the patent trial of the century (Apple sued Samsung for alleged infringement of design patents, software patents and trade dress). Round one went to Apple who was awarded

$1.05 billion. Samsung has of course appealed and Apple's request for injunction has been denied, so they're also appealing. The final decision is most likely still many years away. Meanwhile the race is on.

While that's all very interesting, perhaps the important question for real estate agents today is this: Which Smartphone is best for you? So, let's take a look at a few different things to help make that decision easier for you. We'll evaluate tablets and apps in Chapter 10: *How to Become a Paperless Agent.*

The Top Five

On December 12, 2012, LaptopMag. com published its Best Smartphones of 2012 review. Here is how they ranked the top five along with their brief commentary on each.

1. **iPhone 5:** The iPhone 5 gives Apple fans what they've been waiting for: a bigger screen, 4G LTE and easier Facebook sharing for starters. But it's the design of this phone that makes it truly stand out. Measuring just 0.3 inches thick and weighing a mere 4 ounces, the iPhone 5 is so light and svelte that you really have to hold it in your hands to believe it. This one-hand-friendly handset also boasts one of the sharpest cameras around, a fast A6 chip and more than 7 hours of battery life. Yes, the Maps app is flawed, but otherwise the iPhone 5's combination of

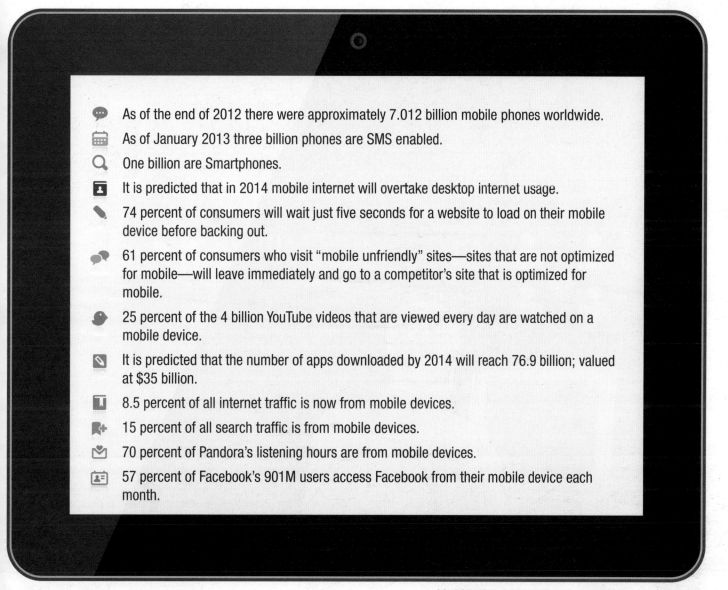

- As of the end of 2012 there were approximately 7.012 billion mobile phones worldwide.
- As of January 2013 three billion phones are SMS enabled.
- One billion are Smartphones.
- It is predicted that in 2014 mobile internet will overtake desktop internet usage.
- 74 percent of consumers will wait just five seconds for a website to load on their mobile device before backing out.
- 61 percent of consumers who visit "mobile unfriendly" sites—sites that are not optimized for mobile—will leave immediately and go to a competitor's site that is optimized for mobile.
- 25 percent of the 4 billion YouTube videos that are viewed every day are watched on a mobile device.
- It is predicted that the number of apps downloaded by 2014 will reach 76.9 billion; valued at $35 billion.
- 8.5 percent of all internet traffic is now from mobile devices.
- 15 percent of all search traffic is from mobile devices.
- 70 percent of Pandora's listening hours are from mobile devices.
- 57 percent of Facebook's 901M users access Facebook from their mobile device each month.

SOURCE MOBILE MARKETING STRATEGIES KNOWLEDGE BANK

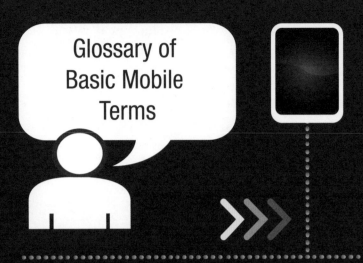

Glossary of Basic Mobile Terms

TABLET: A tablet computer, or simply tablet, is a one-piece mobile computer primarily operated by touchscreen. The user's finger essentially functions as the mouse and cursor, removing the need for the physical hardware components necessary for a desktop or laptop computer. An onscreen, hideable virtual keyboard is also integrated into the display. Available in a variety of sizes, even the smallest touchscreens are much larger than those of a Smartphone or PDA. A tablet computer may be connected to a keyboard with a wireless link or a USB port.

SMARTPHONE: A Smartphone is a mobile phone built on a mobile operating system with more advanced computing capability and connectivity than a standard mobile phone. The first Smartphones combined the functions of a personal digital assistant (PDA) with a mobile phone. Later models added the functionality of portable media players, low-end compact digital cameras, pocket video cameras and GPS navigation units to form one multi-use device. Many modern Smartphones also include high-resolution touchscreens and web browsers that display standard web pages as well as mobile-optimized sites. High-speed data access is provided by Wi-Fi and Mobile Broadband. The mobile operating systems (OS) used by modern Smartphones include Google's Android, Apple's iOS, Nokia's Symbian (nokia.com), RIM's BlackBerry OS, Samsung's Bada (samsung.com), Microsoft's Windows Phone, Hewlett-Packard's (hp.com) webOS and embedded Linux (oracle.com) distributions such as Maemo (maemo.org) and MeeGo (meego.com). Such operating systems can be installed on many different phone models, and typically each device can receive multiple OS software updates over its lifetime.

NETWORK: A mobile network is a radio network distributed over land areas called cells, each served by at least one fixed-location transceiver, known as a cell site or base station. In a cellular network each cell uses a different set of frequencies from neighboring cells to avoid interference and provide guaranteed bandwidth within each cell. When joined together these cells provide radio coverage over a wide geographic area. This enables a large number of portable transceivers (mobile phones, pagers, etc.) to communicate with each other and with fixed transceivers and telephones anywhere in the network, via base stations, even if some of the transceivers are moving through more than one cell during transmission.

SOURCE WIKIPEDIA

ANDROID: A Linux-based operating system designed primarily for touch-screen mobile devices. Initially developed by Android, Inc. (android.com), whom Google financially backed and later purchased in 2005, Android was unveiled in 2007 and the first Android-powered phone was sold in October 2008. It's open source code and permissive licensing allows the software to be freely modified and distributed by device manufacturers, wireless carriers and enthusiast developers. The estimated number of applications downloaded from Google Play (play.google.com), Androids primary App Store, reached 25 billion in September 2012, three years and 11 months after opening. By comparison, Apple's App Store reached 25 billion downloads in just under three years and eight months.

iOS: A mobile operating system developed and distributed by Apple, Inc. It is Apple's mobile version of the OS X operating system used on its computers. Originally released in 2007 for the iPhone and iPod Touch, it has been extended to support other Apple devices such as the iPad and Apple TV. Unlike Microsoft's Windows Phone (Windows CE) and Google's Android, Apple does not license iOS for installation on non-Apple hardware.

As of September 12, 2012, Apple's App Store contained more than 700,000 iOS apps, which have collectively been downloaded more than 30 billion times. iOS had a 14.9 percent share of the Smartphone mobile operating system units shipped in the third quarter of 2012, behind only Google's Android. In June 2012 it accounted for 65 percent of mobile web data consumption (including use on both the iPod Touch and the iPad). By mid-2012 there were 410 million devices activated. According to the special media event held by Apple on September 12, 2012, 400 million devices have been sold through June 2012.

The user interface of iOS is based on the concept of direct manipulation, using multi-touch gestures. Interface control elements consist of sliders, switches and buttons. Interaction includes gestures such as swipe, tap, pinch and reverse pinch, all of which have specific definitions within the context of the operating system and its multi-touch interface. Internal accelerometers are used by some applications to respond to shaking the device (one common result is the undo command) or rotating it in three dimensions (one common result is switching from portrait to landscape mode).

APP: A mobile application (or mobile app) is a software application designed to run on Smartphones, tablet computers and other mobile devices. Apps are available through application distribution platforms, which are typically operated by the owner of the mobile operating system: Apple App Store (store.apple.com), Google Play, Windows Phone Store (windowsphone.com) and BlackBerry App World (us.blackberry.com/apps). Some apps are free, while others have a price. Usually, they are downloaded from the platform to a target device, typically a Smartphone or tablet.

portability, performance, apps and accessories can't be beat.

2. **Samsung Galaxy S lll:** The most innovative Smartphone of the year makes it easier to share everything, whether you're looking to transfer videos between Galaxy phones with a tap or broadcast your photos to an entire group over Wi-Fi. The S III has a ton of other nifty features behind its 4.8-inch HD screen, including Direct Call for dialing a contact just by lifting the phone to your head and Pop up Play for watching a video while you're using another app. While the screen could be brighter, a slim design, swift camera and smooth performance solidify the S III as one of the very best phones of 2102.

3. **Motorola Droid RAZR Maxx HD:** The Droid RAZR Maxx HD is the marathoner of Smartphones. In fact, this Verizon device lasts more than two hours longer than the average Smartphone. We're talking 8 hours and 13 minutes in the LAPTOP Battery Test, which involves continuous Web surfing over 4G LTE. But the Droid RAZR Maxx isn't all about its beefy 3,300 milliamps hours (mAh) battery. It sports a sleek but strong Kevlar-infused design, a very bright and crisp HD display and loud and clear audio. A recent upgrade to Jelly Bean adds welcome enhancements like Google Now and offline voice typing. You'll pay a premium for the Maxx's extra endurance, but it's well worth it.

4. **Nokia Lumia 920:** If you haven't considered a Windows phone, the Lumia 920 will make you a believer. In addition to sporting Microsoft's compelling Live Tile interface, this Windows Phone 8 device features a breakthrough PureView camera that takes some of the best low-light pictures we've seen. Nokia sweetens this $99 steal of an AT&T phone with integrated wireless charging capability and useful and entertaining apps like Nokia Drive and Nokia Music. Although the Lumia 920 is on the hefty side, we love how colors pop off the 4.5-inch screen, as well as the multiple color options for the phone itself.

5. **Samsung Galaxy Note II:** Proving that bigger can be better, the Galaxy Note II makes the most of its enormous 5.5-inch HD display, starting with an S Pen that makes it easy to take

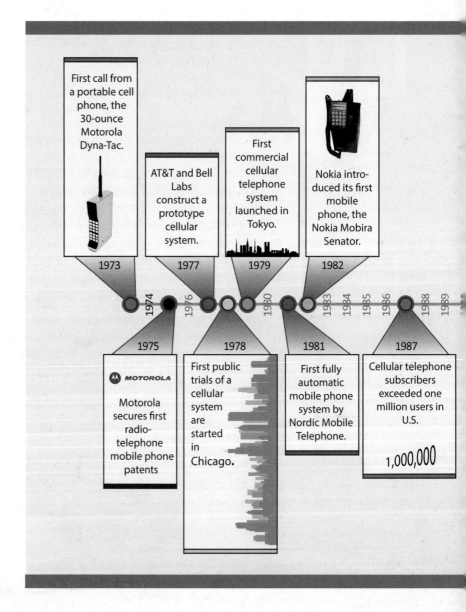

notes and preview emails just by hovering the pen above the screen. It gets better. Samsung's multi-window feature lets you run two applications side by side, so you can surf the Web while you watch YouTube or check Facebook. The Note II is also a powerhouse, thanks to its quad-core Exynos, and lasts more than 9 hours on a charge. Those with smaller hands may want to steer clear, but overall the Note II is

the big-screen to beat.

And nine days later, on December 21, 2012, CNet.com put together their list of the top five Smartphones:

1. **Apple iPhone 5:** The iPhone 5 completely rebuilds the iPhone on a framework of new features and design, addressing its major previous shortcomings. It's absolutely the best iPhone to date, and it easily secures its place

in the top tier of the Smartphone universe.

2. **Samsung Galaxy S III:** Pumped with high-performing hardware and creative software features, the Samsung Galaxy S3 is an excellent, top-end phone that's neck and neck with the HTC One X.

3. **HTC Droid DNA:** With quad-core power, 4G LTE, a lovely 5-inch screen, and a stunning design, the $199.99 HTC Droid DNA is currently Verizon's best Android deal.

4. Motorola Droid RAZR Maxx HD: Motorola's fast, stylish Droid Razr Maxx HD offers outstanding battery life, but its camera captures unimpressive images.

5. Nokia Lumia 920: Nokia's Lumia 920 is heavy and thick, but if you want the most powerful, feature-rich Windows phone available, this is it.

There is a lot of similarity between these two lists, with four of the same Smartphones appearing on each. Currently the Apple iPhone 5 is rated as the best and the Samsung Galaxy S III as the second best on both lists. Both are great Smartphones and will do everything you need them to do.

OTHER FACTORS TO CONSIDER
1. **Availability of Apps**

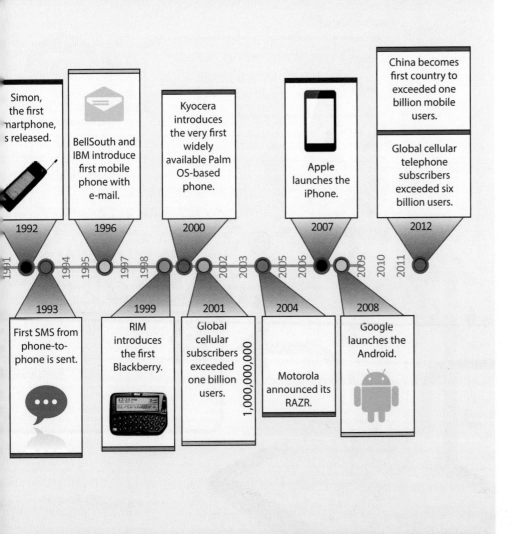

SOURCE REALSURE, INC.

Many developers create apps for Apple's iOS first, as it has a constant and consistent size, shape and code to build for. So many times we hear about a wildly popular app taking an industry by storm, and it's "iOS only." There is a reason for that, and this is a factor you must consider when deciding which Smartphone to purchase.

2. Consistency of Apple

With every generation of the iPhone there is only one device size. It's the same device no matter what carrier offers it and, therefore, it's easy to manage. Because of this physical predictability, many more third-party accessories are built for the iPhone than for the Android. When the iOS software has an upgrade available, it's immediately available across all

similar models.

3. Flash

The iPhone doesn't use Flash. People are sometimes talked out of buying an iPhone because the sales person at the store says, "Don't buy the iPhone, it doesn't use Flash!" In April of 2010 the late Steve Jobs wrote a letter with his thoughts on Flash. Approximately one year later, Adobe agreed and said

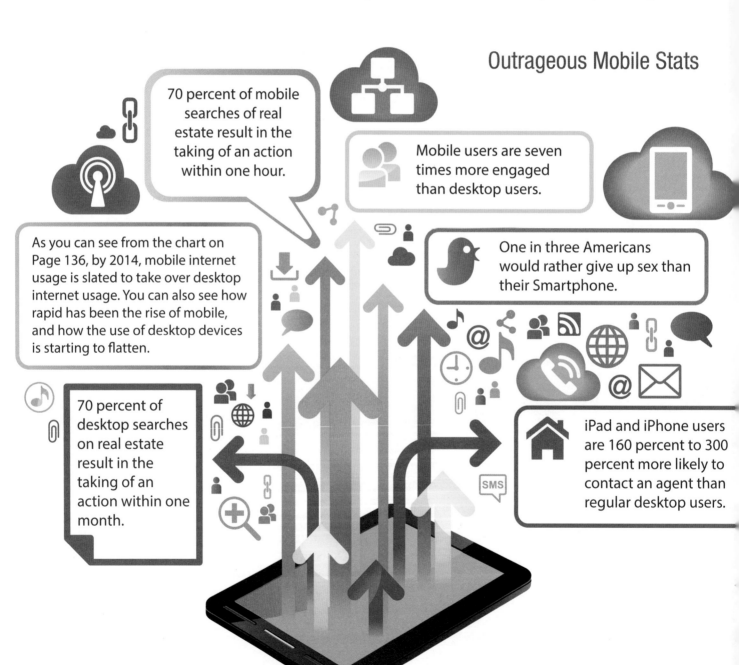

Outrageous Mobile Stats

70 percent of mobile searches of real estate result in the taking of an action within one hour.

Mobile users are seven times more engaged than desktop users.

As you can see from the chart on Page 136, by 2014, mobile internet usage is slated to take over desktop internet usage. You can also see how rapid has been the rise of mobile, and how the use of desktop devices is starting to flatten.

One in three Americans would rather give up sex than their Smartphone.

70 percent of desktop searches on real estate result in the taking of an action within one month.

iPad and iPhone users are 160 percent to 300 percent more likely to contact an agent than regular desktop users.

SOURCE KLEINER PERKINS CAUFIELD & BYERS

Flash wasn't going to move forward as a mobile platform, leaving HTML5 as the frontrunner. Flash was too slow, too clunky and suffered from too many bugs. It just didn't perform well over networks. The bottom line: whether you buy an iPhone or not, don't let "absence of Flash" be the deciding factor," because we believe it's not a legitimate issue at this point as HTML5 is rapidly becoming the standard.

frustration of Android is that in many cases the manufacturer of any given device controls if and when a device is able to upgrade to the latest operating system, so you don't always know what you're buying or what to expect until you've committed.

4G NETWORKS

The media loves to use the term "4G" or "4G LTE," which is short for "Fourth Generation Long Term

major metropolitan markets with the most densely populated areas being supported first. Let's take a closer at the networks by company and keep in mind this information can change daily.

The Providers

Sprint, Verizon and AT&T are all in the midst of developing and expanding their LTE networks, and all three have the same general

---

Mobile is quite likely the most significant device and tool to be introduced during our lifetime.

---

4. Fragmentation of Android

With the open platform of Android, many device manufacturers have rushed to stake their claim in the marketplace. There are literally hundreds of devices, in all different shapes, sizes and price points, with each taking aim at the iPhone's market share. Because of Android's open source platform there are several challenges important to note.

Many of these devices actually operate on different Android platforms. Some statistics show that only two to three percent of Android devices are operating on the newest operating system, called "Ice Cream Sandwich" (as of December 2012), with most operating on predecessor platforms such as "Jelly Bean," "Gingerbread" and others on even older platforms. This creates huge fragmentation within the Android sphere. Another

Evolution." In theory, LTE can support download speeds of up to 100Mbps and upload speeds of up to 50Mbps, but all you really need to know is that it's faster than current 3G technologies—in fact, up to 10 times faster than 3G.

So, who really has the bigger, faster network? It all depends on where you live and the infrastructure in place in that market. Certain salespeople have been known to say some phones are actually inferior because they're not 4G. Whether or not a phone is 4G capable only makes a difference if there is 4G available in that market. Having said that, there is a big difference between true 4G and 3G but, in many cases, this point is for the most part moot, as certain markets may not see good widespread 4G deployments for years. The build out of 4G starts in the

goal: offer as much coverage to as many people as possible. So, the smart move is simple: buy the best phone available on the best network available in your market. In the majority of cases that will probably be either Verizon or AT&T. Having said that, here is a short summary of the top three primary providers (in alphabetical order):

1. AT&T: Their LTE network covers 109 markets as of this writing and expects its rollout to be complete by the end of 2013. What AT&T currently lacks in rollout it makes up for in speed, at least according to PCWorld (pcworld.com). The publication found that download transfer speeds on AT&T's network averaged at 9.56 Mbps, which was a tad higher than the 7.35 Mbps speeds on Verizon's network.

2. Sprint: Having decided to scrap its WiMAX efforts in 2011, Sprint's LTE network is, predictably, still in early development stages. Sprint says it intends for its LTE network to cover 250 million users by the end of 2013. That's all well and good, but the fact remains that Sprint's LTE network has a long way to go, and when it does get going it will do so in a fairly limited fashion.

3. Verizon: As of the date of this writing Verizon states that its 4G LTE network covers 470 cities and nearly 80 percent of the U.S. population. Currently, the carrier offers over 20 4G LTE-ready devices, including eleven Smartphones, a half dozen tablets, a handful of mobile hotspots and a pair of notebooks.

MOBILE PHOTOGRAPHY

One of the most important aspects of marketing a property is quality photography. As a result, many successful agents report that the best money spent in marketing begins with professional photography and/or videography. The visual is everything. It's a home's first impression and the best chance of online engagement. Both clients and consumers alike want to see good photography and they always want more pictures.

Today almost all Smartphones have cameras with five to 10 megapixel-quality, making them as good as or better than your regular digital camera, but not as good as a DSLR camera. And with a plethora of available apps to edit, take full panoramic photos, re-color, crop, resize, add lighting, zoom and add effects, Smartphones have for many become the preferred camera of choice. Mobile photography has become a very convenient way to take picture of houses.

Nearly every home could benefit from added lighting and one of the downfalls of Smartphone photography is taking quality photos in low light conditions. And, unfortunately, Smartphone Flash is typically average at best.

Everything looks better when lit properly and you can add lighting with lighting kits, and much like a DSLR, you can add an off camera flash. And although it's not recommended for home photography, you can find a variety of add on lenses for the iPhone, like the OLLOCLIP, (available on olloclip.com or amazon.com) which adds a macro lens for close up photography, a fish eye and a

Global Mobile vs. Desktop Internet User Projection

Internet Users (mm)

2000 · 1600 · 1200 · 800 · 400

2007 2008 2009 2010 2011 2012 2013 2014 2015

2007-2015

～ Desktop Internet Users
≋ Mobile Internet Users

SOURCE MORGAN STANLEY, YAHOO MOBILE SHOPPING FRAMEWORK, NIELSON RESEARCH wide angle lens. Check out photojojo. com for great accessories and HDHat, which offers a wide range of add-ons for Smartphones, including special lenses, stabilization and lighting kits, etc.

When it comes to the processing of the photos, most of the editing can be done on the devices themselves. While serious Photographers might prefer serious programs like PhotoShop (adobe.com/photoshopfamily), Lightroom (adobe.com/lightroom) or Aperture (apple.com/aperture), most users will do just fine with the apps available on the phone. You can now even edit video on mobile devices; iMovie is available on the iPhone and iPad and a version of Final Cut Pro is available on the iPad.

touch you can use to capture photos instantly with some great controls, add cool effects and share them with your Facebook, Twitter or Flickr friends on-the-fly.

- **Camera Awesome** - The app is more flexible than Apple's native camera function, providing extra control over focus and exposure. Along with enhancements including a level to assist in composition, high speed drive modes and an anti-shake mode to help avoid blurry pictures, Camera Awesome offers in-app photo enhancement and filtering, and ties into a variety of photo sharing services.

ratio typically used by mobile device cameras.

- **Snapseed** (recently purchased by Google) - The Snapseed photo editor is a one-stop app for performing both quick and in-depth edits on a mobile device or computer.

- **FrameMagic for Collages** - This app creates collages from photos.

- **Over & Overgram for adding Text** - This app adds beautiful typography to Instagram photos.

- **Pixeet** - This app allows the creation of stunning 360° "Google Street View" like virtual tours within your iPhone or iPad. Share your

Google's Android phones and Apple's iPhone now control 89 percent of the market according to comScore, up from 51% only two years ago.

STAND OUT APPS FOR MOBILE PHOTOGRAPHY

- **Pro HDRProCamera** - This app creates well-exposed full-resolution pictures captured with the phone's camera and from already stored pictures. Therefore two or three pictures with different exposures are stitched into one HDR image.

- **Camera+** - Camera Plus is a free camera app for the iPhone 4, 3GS, 3G and iPod

- **Instagram** - This is an online photo-sharing and social networking service that enables its users to take pictures, apply digital filters to them, and share them on a variety of social networking services, such as media sites including Facebook or Twitter. A distinctive feature is that it confines photos to a square shape, similar to Kodak Instamatic and Polaroid images, in contrast to the 4:3 aspect

panoramas on the Internet, social networks or corporate portals in one click from your iPhone.

- **NightCap** - This app adjusts photo exposure and captures up to 15x more light than any other app.

- **PhotoToaster** - This is a top rated photo editor for the iPhone and iPad.

- **PhotoShop Express** - This is a more simplistic version of

From the Vault: Real Estate Confronts Reality (1997)

"The cellular phone may soon emerge as the ideal Internet access tool and could even displace computers as the Web-connection of choice by 2005."

the sophisticated PhotoShop photo editing software.

- **TouchRetouch** - This is an app that lets you remove unwanted content or objects from your photos, using just your finger and iPhone or iPod Touch.

- **iPhoto** - This is Apple's native photography app which contains basic editing functionalities.

OPTIMIZING FOR MOBILE

Another topic that should be addressed in the larger mobile conversation is optimizing your website for mobile devices. As web access from mobile devices is expected to overtake web access from desktop devices sometime during 2014, here are some things to think about:

1. Mobile Version of Your Site

First, your site must be "mobilized," but not all mobile sites are created equally. So, even after deciding to make your site "mobile friendly," you still need to make sure that it's done correctly. Some mobile sites look good on your device and a few others, but that isn't a guarantee it will look good on ALL mobile devices. So, the first question for you to ask your mobile website provider is this: "Will

this mobile website work on ALL (or almost ALL) mobile devices and will it OPTIMIZE to every screen size and shape?"

2. Load Time

Studies have shown that consumers only give a mobile website several seconds to load and if the content doesn't fit, looks too small or even seems remotely confusing, back they go and on to another site or search. So, load time is crucial.

3. Keyword Phrases

On Mobile devices many consumers use shorter keyword phrases due to

the not-always-convenient typing experience applicable to most Smartphones. Also, they tend to be more reliant on Google's auto-complete feature for search. Keep this in mind when optimizing meta tags, titles and descriptions.

4. Size Matters

On touchscreen devices, small buttons or links usually are not convenient. And many consumers struggle to touch the appropriate buttons. Larger, clearer, simpler buttons are better.

5. Being Visual

Be sure photos are being optimized for the device and are tagged accordingly. Photos that are not optimized for mobile can slow the load process considerably.

SUMMARY

Mobile has, probably more than any other invention during our lifetime, redefined how we live in our world. Smartphones have reshaped the way we do business. Living without the mobile Smartphone is, for most people, no longer an option.

So, one of the most important things you can do as a real estate professional is to adopt the latest and most advanced mobile systems and strategies you can handle. You must educate yourself and stay current. Your annual reading of the *Swanepoel TECHNOLOGY Report* will go a long way toward keeping you current with respect to the changes, strategies and best practices surrounding mobile.

Mobile improves communication, search, marketing, transactions and speed of delivery, and allows for better presentations, better service, and more, faster data. And those are exactly the things it's going to take to serve the client of today, and certainly the client of tomorrow. Your clients probably already have access to most of the same data and apps that you do. They're already surfing the web 24/7 from anywhere and anytime of the day. You don't want your clients to do your job for you, know more about real estate than you or have easier access to everything than you do.

Mobile is one of the most important tools you have as a real estate professional. Master it well as your career may very well depend on it.

very strong incom

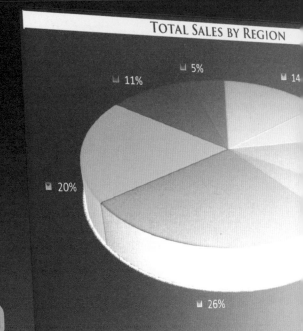

TOTAL SALES BY REGION

☐ 5%   ☐ 11%   ☐ 14

☐ 20%

☐ 26%

☐ Oil ☐ Gas ☐ Electric power ☐ Medicine ☐ Textile

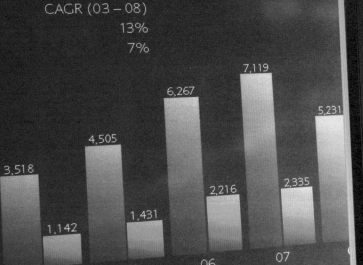

CAGR (03 – 08)
13%
7%

	7,119
6,267	5,231
4,505	
3,518	2,335
2,216	
1,431	
1,142	

04   05   06   07

s of total income   H1 08

nt... in 2013

ncome   4,784
                                   (2,225)
ome   852
arket losses in income
dit   3,411
                                   (1,226)
ome
ent charges and other credit provisions
                                   2,185
ne

TOTAL SALES BY REGION
REGION SALES

Region			Sales
West	⊗	€	1 236 345,0	C
South	✓	€	1 896 354,0	S
North	!	€	2 569 345,0	C
East	!	€	1 893 543,0	S
Total		€	7 595 587,0	

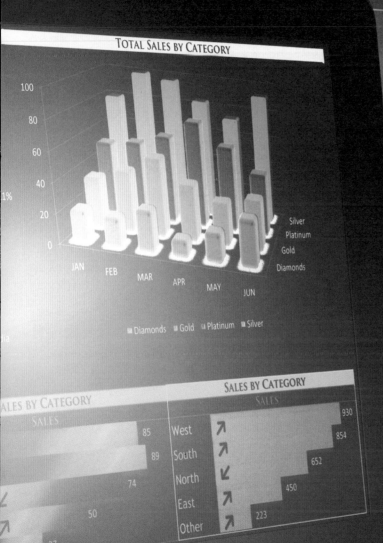

How To Become A
Paperless Agent

Tablets: The Real Estate Professionals' Best Friend

How To Become A Paperless Agent

The home purchase transaction is the most complicated and financially complex transaction the average person will ever be a part of, and it's also always been one of the most "paper intensive" activities you can think of. From buyer tour packets to CMAs for sellers to disclosures for buyers to purchase offers to mortgage packages and closing documents, from start to finish, the real estate process is one large stack of documents after another. And while this natural dependence on paper has always made sense because it was the only option available up until recently, times have changed and in today's digital world this approach is no longer the most efficient or cost-effective way to serve buyers and sellers.

Almost everything we do today can be done digitally; paying bills, reading the newspaper or a favorite book, watching a movie, playing games, talking or emailing with a loved one across the country or even on the other side of the world—the list is almost literally infinite. So it's most certainly time to complete the entire real estate transaction digitally as well.

No matter where you are today, everything you need to conduct a transaction is now digitally at your fingertips. In this new digital age, conducting transactions without relying on paper does away with many of the inefficiencies of traditional practices. For example, a pre-listing packet no longer has to be printed, stuffed into an envelope and sent via snail mail. It can now be emailed to a potential seller to be viewed before the listing appointment. Getting a signature no longer requires a trip back to the office. Agents have the capability to obtain a signature digitally. A counteroffer can be sent electronically and that means—once again—no trip back to the office to print out a document, annotate it and fax it back to the appropriate parties.

In Chapter 9 we discussed the revolutionary growth of the mobile device and the extent to which it has altered society in general and the home buying transaction in particular. In this chapter we continue the journey and focus specifically on the huge contribution tablets have made and continue to make in the real estate transaction.

Collectively, the Mobile revolution (Smartphones, Tablets and Apps) will forever revolutionize the home buying transaction.

REINVENTING THE HOME BUYING TRANSACTION

Real estate sales, as opposed to many other industries and professions, is inherently mobile and hence ideally suited to maximize the structure and mobile benefits of tablets. Both homebuyers and the agents who represent them constantly drive around when they're looking at houses. With very little time actually being spent at one fixed location, such as a real estate office, a tablet provides the paperless functionality of an office anywhere, anytime.

So, if you wish to become a paperless agent, here are the five simple steps to transition from conducting real estate transactions traditionally to doing business digitally:

Step 1: Get an iPad: Get (if you don't already have one) a tablet. We recommend the iPad 3 or newer, with at least 16 gigabytes of memory and 3G or 4G capabilities (see more on alternative tablet options below).

Step 2: Get the Apps: To successfully complete a traditional transaction requires a diverse and large selection of tools, such as contract, pen and paper, files, filing cabinets, calendars, traditional computers, printers and scanners, etc. With the paperless transaction you still need to do the same basic activities, but now you'll be doing them digitally. Beyond the iPad, the new tools that allow you to do this are called apps (applications), and each app is designed to perform a specific function that is typically quite narrow in scope. We'll be discussing which specific apps you need to obtain later in this chapter.

Step 3: Learn: Make a pledge to yourself to learn how to use the iPad and these applications. Becoming skilled at anything requires time and effort, and becoming a master at mobile technology is no different. The commitment must be made to move forward and embrace this new way of doing things, rather than falling back into doing

them the same way you always have.

Step 4: Master the Process: Practice and refine your skills in using these apps on a regular basis. Millions of people around the globe have an iPad, but most don't know how to use it to its maximum efficiency as a business tool. As the old saying goes, practice makes perfect! It takes time to master paperless transactions, using the selected apps and the processes and systems outlined here to fully leverage the iPad's potential when working with buyers and sellers.

Step 5: Stay Current: Constantly learn and grow as mobile technology evolves. Users no longer have the luxury of time to master a new skill set or a new set of apps. Neither do you have the comfort of thinking that once a skill has been learned that you will be able to use it for a long time. Another fallacy is that the app or skill you're using will be the same version, let alone the same app or technology,

you used last year. Technology keeps evolving, and a key to having success with your tablet is understanding that this process is very dynamic.

BEST TABLETS
Here are the tablets consistently rated the highest, according to PCMag.com:

1. iPad 4: Now in its fourth iteration in two years, the Apple iPad continues its reign as the best large tablet you can buy today. The 4th Generation iPad has it all: top performance, a stellar screen, a surprisingly good camera, speedy Wi-Fi and a breathtaking library of spectacular apps. Unlike other 10-inch tablets on the market, it's the full package, which makes it a very rare five-star product.

2. iPad Mini: If you want those iPad-exclusive apps and price is no object, then no other small-screen tablet will do. Beautifully made, slim and light, the iPad mini packs precisely the

Vendors	4Q11 Market Share	4Q11 Shipments (in millions)	4Q12 Market Share	4Q12 Shipments (in millions)	4Q11/4Q12 Growth (Shipments)
Apple	51.70%	15.5	43.60%	22.9	48.10%
Samsung	7.30%	2.2	15.10%	7.9	263.00%
Amazon.com	15.90%	4.7	11.50%	6	26.80%
ASUS	2.00%	0.6	5.80%	3.1	402.30%
Barnes & Noble	4.60%	1.4	1.90%	1	-27.70%
Others	18.50%	5.5	22.10%	11.6	108.90%
All Vendors	100%	29.9	100%	52.5	75.30%

Top 5 Tablet Vendors with Market Share and Shipments

SOURCE INTERNATIONAL DATA CORPORATION

power of an iPad 2 into a tablet you'll actually want to carry around.

3. Google Nexus 7: This one is a game-changer. The Nexus 7 is the first tablet with Android 4.1 "Jelly Bean" and it's the most bang for the buck you can get in the market right now. It's versatile, well-built, fast and

its 1,920 by 1,200-pixel resolution is still pretty impressive. Aside from the screen, the TF700 looks and feels a lot like the Asus Eee Pad Transformer Prime TF201, but inside there are slightly more powerful components, from a faster-clocked processor to an improved camera. It's a major step forward for Android tablets,

majority of existing software made for Windows 7 and XP.

The Bottom Line
There are so many choices. Different price points, sizes, manufacturers, operating systems, etc. The first thing to do is decide if you like the open source platform. If you like

---

Real estate sales, as opposed to many other industries and professions, is inherently mobile and hence ideally suited to maximize the structure and mobile benefits of tablets.

---

a lot of fun to use. It basically renders every 7-inch tablet priced at more than $300 pretty much irrelevant. If you're looking for a small tablet to surf the Internet and play games, this is the one to buy.

4. Samsung Galaxy Note 10.1: The Galaxy Note 10.1 is the first tablet to actually change my workflow. It's the only 10-inch Android tablet with clear consumer advantages over the iPad. It's sure to become a cult classic for its three killer apps: split-screen note-taking, pressure-sensitive drawing and a universal living-room remote control. Those features elevate it above other Android models to make it best for large-screen tablets.

5. Asus Transformer Pad Infinity: The New Apple iPad started the resolution race, and it looks like Asus is the first to market with an Android contender—the Asus Transformer Pad Infinity TF700. It doesn't quite match the iPad pixel-for-pixel, but

but just not enough apps that take full advantage of the high-resolution screen yet.

6. Microsoft Surface: The Microsoft Surface with Windows RT is their first entry into the wild world of tablets. Priced to compete with the Apple iPad, the Surface tablet with 64GB of storage comes with a 10.6-inch, five-point multi-touch screen. As is, it's aimed at users that want to do more than simply consume media and websites, with innovative keyboard covers that make some of the more expensive Windows 8 tablets' docking solutions look absolutely clunky by comparison. It feels like a "real computer" and comes with a full copy of Microsoft Office 2013 (Home and Student Edition). Thanks to Microsoft's Windows RT operating system the Surface has the same user interface as upcoming Windows 8 laptops and tablets. However, since it uses Windows RT and a more economical ARM processor, the Surface isn't compatible with the

having tons of choices, operating systems and prices, you are more likely an Android buyer. If you're more comfortable with consistency, a huge selection of accessories, a user experience that is very similar between devices and a more robust app store—and you're willing to pay a little bit more—you're probably more an iPad (or iPad mini) user.

But this shouldn't deter you from moving forward with any of these products. Far more important than WHICH tablet you use is simply THAT you use a tablet. That said, as Apple currently reigns supreme (100 million units sold in 30 months after its April 2010 debut), we have in this Report focused on the iPad as the current "mobile weapon of choice."

MAJOR PAPERLESS PLAYERS
Here is a quick overview of the more significant current players in the "paperless" industry, in alphabetical order. We suggest you visit the websites of these providers to gain

more information about the services of each, as these technologies often evolve.

Authentisign

The Authentisign system (by MRIS.com) automatically routes documents, gathers signatures and distributes fully executed documents once all parties have signed. And it's "foolproof signing," since regular signature blocks must be signed in order for it to be considered complete. Signers can't miss a signature or initial block. You can also add reviewers in addition to the signers so agents and attorneys can review documents before they are presented to clients for signature.

Cartavi

Cartavi (cartavi.com) is a simple way to securely collaborate on documents with everyone involved in the process transaction. Cartavi gives you one place to conveniently store, manage and share the documents that support your transactions, from your desktop or on the go. Cartavi has a feature called "Transaction Rooms," which allows for quick access to and storage of documents for everyone involved in a transaction. "My Docs" ensures private storage for secure documents, and there are different permissions to allow who in your network can see what. In each transaction room, clients can electronically sign and send back documents because Cartavi is integrated with DocuSign. Cartavi has mobile apps for iPad, iPhone and Android.

DocuSign/DocuSign Ink

DocuSign (docusign.com) and DocuSign Ink (the mobile version) is an app that allows users to e-sign documents on tablets and Smartphones. From PDFs to Microsoft Office documents to image files to faxes to just about anything, DocuSign Ink converts most every kind of file and allows for legally-binding signatures anywhere, thereby eliminating traditional printing, faxing and scanning of paper documents. Signers can provide their documents via upload. When using the full version of DocuSign, tags can be added on each document to specifically direct people where to sign and initial remotely. Agents can also set the sequence of signing and set reminders and expirations for each form.

DotLoop

DotLoop (dotloop.com) is a cloud-based technology that includes e-signature capabilities like DocuSign/DocuSign Ink, along with document storage capabilities like Cartavi. With DotLoop you select who you want "in the loop" on a given transaction and use permissions to allow and disallow access to people, much like you can with Cartavi. The primary difference between DotLoop and DocuSign is that, with DotLoop, people access documents by creating accounts, whereas with DocuSign and DocuSign Ink, no account creation is required.

Interesting Tablet Statisitcs

- 11 percent of adults already own some version of a tablet computer.

- Three-in-ten tablet users say they now spend more time consuming news than they did before purchasing their tablet.

- Daily use includes: email (54 percent), consuming news (53 percent), social networking (39 percent), reading books (27 percent) and watching movies (13 percent).

- 77 percent use their tablets every day for an average of 90 minutes.

- Tablet news users say they prefer tablets over traditional computers, print publications or television as a way to get quick news headlines and to read long-form pieces.

Zipform

ZipForm 6 (zipform.com) by zipLogix is the exclusive and official forms software of NAR. This easy-to-use forms software is designed to increase the real estate professional's productivity and help complete contracts more efficiently, all while reducing risk.

Said Krisstina Wise, CEO of the GoodLife Team: "We find that combining the highly-specialized and intuitive technologies of zipForm, DocuSign and Cartavi in a simple and sequential order helps our agents to easily use the mobile apps on their iPads to have the buyers and sellers sign all their documents and then collaborate with all parties of the transaction...all mobile and all on the iPad!"

THE GREAT ENABLER

The term "app" has become so universally popular that in 2010 it was listed as "Word of the Year" by the American Dialect Society. Apps were originally offered for general productivity and information retrieval, but their functionality has expanded dramatically beyond that. The popularity of mobile apps continues to rise as their usage becomes increasingly prevalent across the majority of mobile devices. Think of them as specialized problem-solving tools. Most are limited to a specific functionality and task and are therefore usually easy to learn and use. Apps help you to complete tasks faster, easier and cheaper, and in many cases without paper.

It's hard to believe, but the PC has now been around for 40 years of commercial use. During that time the total number of applications created for the PC reached 75,000. That's a lot, and for decades this defined the context of what was possible with apps. By comparison, however, the number of mobile apps developed between 2006 - 2012 soared to over 1.5 million, according to CNET news (news/cnet.com). As of December 2012 ABI Research (abiresearch.com) estimated that Apple stills leads the pack with 775,000 iOS apps, followed by Google with 612,000 for Droid phones and Microsoft and RIM with 120,000 apps each. However, the number of Android apps is expected to surpass Apple in 2013, becoming the first store in the world to offer over one million apps.

In five years the Apple App Store has shown us how quickly the world can change by becoming the most successful software marketplace the world has ever seen. An estimated 30 million apps are being downloaded every day, transforming mobile phones into ever increasing Smartphones, GPS systems, Productivity Tools and Entertainment Platforms. International Data Corporation (IDC; idc.com) predicts that the total number of global app downloads will surpass 75 billion next year, with a value exceeding $35 billion. This is a huge new world!

BEST APPS FOR REAL ESTATE

So, out of the hundreds of thousands of apps, how do you know which ones to use as a real estate professional? Odds are good that you don't. It's difficult and the population of potential alternatives is constantly changing. To help you with this challenge, we created that list for you. We did this by looking at the home buying process, as well as many other normal activities that agents do, from their point of view. We came up with this list of the best apps currently being

used by tablet-savvy agents who are heavily leveraging their iPads to do some, or in some cases all, of their real estate transactions paperlessly right now. In alphabetical order and with a short description of each, the apps or type of apps you need are as follows:

1. Better Voicemail

This app is a VOIP (voice over Internet protocol) system that is seriously customizable with a user-friendly dashboard interface and all kinds of bells and whistles. If you can't answer a call, you can set up the system to take a message, give address info, transfer to an admin or text back a seller's disclosures—the possibilities are endless.

2. Calendar

Calendar is an app that's native to the iPad. It's a great tool to keep your appointments organized and it should be used from beginning to end on every transaction. You can easily set appointments to show homes, add a buyer consultation appointment, keep precise time records of scheduled showings, keep track of appointment details and stay on track during buyer tours using its map hyperlink functionality.

3. Camscanner

This app allows you use your mobile device to "scan" documents, make minor adjustments with cropping and image quality and digitize documents quickly while in the field.

4. Cartavi

Your offer was accepted and now it's time to manage all the related documents with all parties involved

Basic Steps to Becoming A Paperless Agent

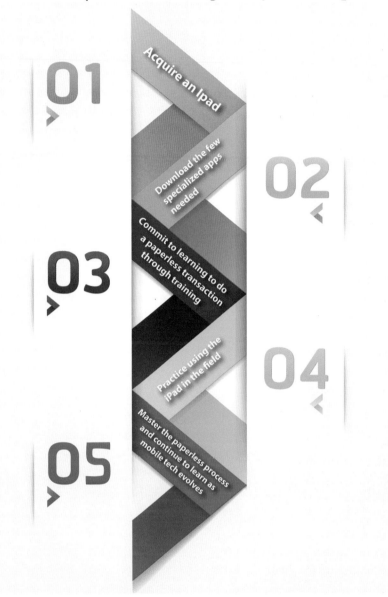

01 Acquire an Ipad

02 Download the few specialized apps needed

03 Commit to learning to do a paperless transaction through training

04 Practice using the iPad in the field

05 Master the paperless process and continue to learn as mobile tech evolves

SOURCE THE GOODLIFE TEAM

in the transaction. Cartavi allows all documents to be stored and shared with the lender, the buyer or seller, the title company and any other party that needs access to them during the transaction. This means having ready access to every document germane to the transaction at any time.

5. DocuSign

Once an offer is written and you require a signature, it's time for DocuSign. This app enables you to obtain electronic initials and signatures on the offer as well as on any other documents related to the transaction. A buyer can sign an offer while still sitting in the living room of the house she has fallen in love with and wants to buy, potentially getting an offer in before anyone else does on an in-demand property.

6. Evernote

Evernote is an amazing tool for staying organized. It allows the sharing of Notes and Notebooks, syncing with your desktop and other devices and leveraging the power and convenience of cloud-based storage for large quantities of files. It's the perfect place to keep detailed records about every buying client, e.g., notes from your initial buyer consultation, checklists, tax records, property photos, audio and video recordings and any other pertinent information related to the transaction with that customer (for more expanded details on Evernote see Chapter 7).

You can also use Evernote while at a listing appointment to capture information about the seller and the house exactly like you did during your initial consultation with the buyer. In addition to capturing written information, you can also use the video tool in Evernote to digitally capture the important features of the home. Assuming the seller agrees to list with you, you can then turn around and use those images and/or video to create marketing materials. And again, all this information can be captured and kept in an Evernote Note specific to that seller, easily accessed when the need arises from any mobile or desktop device.

7. iAnnotate PDF

You've submitted a buyer's offer and the seller quickly responds with a counteroffer. Now, rather than having to drive back to the office, print out a new document, make the updates and/or changes, turn around and scan or fax it back to all interested parties, you can make the annotations digitally on your iPad with iAnnotate PDF, an app that allows digital annotation on electronic documents. Once the annotations have been made, the updated digital document can then be sent back quickly, facilitating a speedy reply and expediting the transaction process.

8. iBooks

Traditionally, buyer tour information is typically printed out and placed on a clipboard or stapled as a packet and given to the buyer. Now, rather than handing the buyer a clipboard stacked with paper, you can simply hand them an iPad with the same information digitally displayed in a clear, powerful way. To do this, instead of printing your buyer tour to paper, simply "print to PDF" (an option available on most every printer), and then drag that PDF onto your iPad. Voila—instant paperless buyer tour packet! Alternatively you can email that same PDF to the client for their records while storing a copy in their Evernote Note for future reference.

When talking listing price with sellers, you can use the iBooks app to take them through your CMA data, showing them the traditional information, e.g., listing, pending and comparable sales information. You prepare this information just like you do for your buyer tours, creating

Top 5 Tablet Lists....

PC Magazine

1. iPad4
2. Samsung Galaxy Note 10.1
3. Amazon Kindle Fire HD
4. Asus Transformer Pad Infinity
5. Microsoft Surface

TechRadar

1. iPad Mini
2. iPad 4
3. Google Nexus 7
4. Google Nexus 10
5. Asus Transformer Pad Infinity

your normal CMAs and printing them to PDF instead of to paper, and then adding them to your iPad. This allows you and the seller to quickly review all of the comparable listing information together when determining listing price.

sellers in real time, right when they want answers, allowing for a logical, informed decision.

10. Keynote
Before going on a listing appointment you can share your pre-listing

level as well as a likely decrease in the chance of cold feet on the drive back to the office to submit an offer. Or, in the case where the buyer isn't comfortable with the payment, all parties involved know right away and you potentially cut down on time and

> **Far more important than WHICH tablet you use is simply THAT you use a tablet.**

9. iSwifter
Assuming the mortgage payment estimate turns out to the client's liking (see Mortgage Payment Calculator app below), you can continue the process toward submitting an offer. And you can do that by determining a possible offer price by performing a buyer market analysis. Rather than having to make a trip or a call back to the office you can use the iSwifter app to browse the MLS without worrying about incompatible flash content (which is a problem for many agents with many MLSs) and create a buyer market analysis while still on tour.

If your sellers have additional questions about pricing you can also use iSwifter to browse the MLS and perform whatever additional pricing research may be required, all without ever having to make extra trips or calls back to the office. Additionally, doing this could potentially save extended haggling over price, because you can easily access and quickly present information to the

information with a potential seller. Keynote is a presentation app (similar to PowerPoint) that can be used to create, animate and customize a pre-listing presentation. This pre-listing presentation, containing a story in slide, photo and/or video formats, can then be emailed to the seller. Doing this amps up the experience for the seller and saves the time and money you previously spent on printing, envelope stuffing and postage. You can also use Keynote to create and finalize your listing presentation for the in-person appointment.

11. Mortgage Payment Calculator
A buyer has found a house she loves, but she's not sure if she can afford it. While still at the house you can perform an estimated mortgage calculation right there on the spot. You simply input all the relevant information (offer price, down payment, tax information, HOA fees, etc.), and then share the results with the buyer, who will then have an idea of what her payment will be. This will lead to an increase in her comfort

frustration by getting to that answer quicker and more efficiently.

12. Numbers
After your sellers have decided on a list price, it's time to crunch some numbers to ensure that they fully understand the complete financial ramifications of their decision. The Numbers app can now be used to create a net sheet to show them exactly where they'll stand at various pricing points at and below the list price. Instead of having to go back to the office to calculate all pertinent numbers and email the net sheet, this information can be calculated while still sitting with the sellers at their dining room table.

13. Open Home Pro
Once the house is properly staged and on the market, it's time to hold an open house. You can use Open Home Pro to collect information about potential buyers who tour the home and then follow up with them to assess their potential interest. It's a beautiful info gathering experience,

designed to break the ice at open houses. You can set up each of your listings in the app with a gorgeous interface and custom questions, and it can be used to gather client or agent info feedback. This iOS only app is set up to help you share your listings directly to Facebook, Craigslist and within the Open Home Pro community.

14. Photo

While still touring with the buyer, the Photo app—another app native to the iPad—can be used in tandem with Evernote. This app, used to browse, edit and share photos, provides a visual representation

that have sold. Now there is a way to visually represent how staging works without having to spend so much time and energy convincing the sellers it's the right thing to do.

15. Sign My Pad

This is an app that enables you to sign PDFs and contracts on the go.

16. Skitch

Whenever possible a master salesperson will always illustrate a point visually if they can, rather than just talking about it. The Skitch screen capture and annotation app helps you illustrate concepts to customers. For example, if your buyers are unfamiliar

it right at that point as opposed to pricing it too high in the beginning and dropping the price when traffic has dropped. As an added bonus, Skitch syncs with Evernote, making it simple to save all custom notes made on Skitch into a client's Evernote file.

17. Spotify

Another effective tool is the music app Spotify. You can use it to set the tone for a buyer tour by finding out your client's musical preferences and playing them while driving around viewing properties. This may make the buyer more at ease, thus making the tour a more relaxed and more personalized experience for the client.

The term "app" has become so universally popular that in 2010 it was listed as "Word of the Year" by the American Dialect Society.

---

during the decision-making process, reminding a buyer which home had the most features that matched their buying criteria. They say a picture is worth a thousand words, and in real estate that is absolutely the case. You can take photos and load them directly into that buyer's Note and then share those photos with the client.

You may also leverage Photo to talk about staging. For this conversation you can visually demonstrate how homes that are staged generally sell more quickly than those that aren't. This app can be used to show "before and after" photos of staged homes

with the neighborhood where they're making an offer, you can use Skitch to highlight key locations on a map in their potential new neighborhood; schools, churches, the grocery store, the gym, etc. We have become a very visual society and Skitch is a tool that can definitely be used to help make points visually rather than by text or the spoken word.

When working with sellers on determining a list price, the Skitch app is great for answering common pricing questions. With Skitch you can visually demonstrate how a listing gets the most traffic right after it's listed, and why it's smart to price

18. ZipForms

Once the buyer is ready to make an offer you can digitally access the appropriate standard contract forms, complete the agreement online and even present an offer directly from the home using the ZipForm app. When working with sellers, once they've agreed to list with you, you can produce the listing agreement immediately using this tool.

CASE STUDIES

Fennemore Craig, Arizona's oldest law firm now has its 400 employees transmit, upload, annotate and capture signatures on all pertinent documents online as well as archiving

---

From the Vault: Real Estate Confronts Reality (1997)

"Thanks to the Internet, the confines of time and space are disappearing. Gone are most previous boundaries, creating a new "virtual nation" where the stores have no doors and the malls no walls."

all information digitally. This has eliminated the need for physical storage space and resulted in more disputes being settled more quickly.

Another example is the world's second largest airline, United Airlines that now has their 11,000 pilots use iPads in the cockpit instead of paper charts and maps. This has resulted in an estimated saving of 16 million sheets of paper per year.

Austin-based boutique residential real estate brokerage GoodLife Team, with 25 employees and 250 transactions per year, uses iPads in almost every facet of the home buying transaction. "Our entire sales force uses iPad," says Krisstina Wise, CEO and Founder of GoodLife Team. "By using iPad we're able to rapidly respond to offers and counteroffers, win a home for our clients more effectively and, without question, more efficiently." With an enhanced level of customer service, the company estimates a timesaving's of about three hours per transaction, saving an estimated 750 hours per year. In 2010 the company was selected the "Most Innovative Brokerage" by INMAN News and is even featured on Apple.com because of its well-known use of the iPad in every aspect of its business.

FROM THE CONSUMERS POINT OF VIEW

Homebuyers are also embracing mobile real estate apps in a big way. Apps have opened a whole new world for them, enabling them to be more informed and, in some regards, removed the need to reach out to real estate professionals, at least during the early stages of search. With a huge amount of apps relating to home buying, searching, maps, valuations, community, video tours, etc. available, the consumer of today has become considerably more knowledgeable about certain aspects of the real estate process before reaching out to a real estate broker or agent. Most of these apps are free and their usage has grown exponentially during the last three years. For example, as of early 2013 more homes on Zillow were being viewed on a mobile device than on desktop computers, and in January 2013 that number equated to 202 million homes being viewed on Zillow Mobile—that's a rate of 75 homes per second.

Real Estate Apps for Consumers

As a savvy real estate professional you must have a good understanding of the most popular real estate apps your consumers are using. And we feel that you shouldn't waste your time and energy worrying about whether

you provide better or more accurate information than they do. That's not the debate here, and it's really irrelevant. What is relevant is that consumers—and probably most all of your clients—are using these apps in massive numbers. The following apps have very wide appeal and are being used to educate, influence and direct potential clients. You should know what they offer and what consumers will see on them if they are able to access your listings using them. That will make you a better and more effective real estate professional.

1. HomeSnap

This interesting app is offered by Sawbuck and is currently only available for the iOS platform. Snap a photo of any home and get current or recent listing information, sold data, public tax data or an estimate of value. HomeSnap accesses information from various public sources and allows for editing of the database, so expect some variation in data accuracy. This concept is truly amazing.

2. Realtor.com

Yet another great tool is the Realtor. com app. It allows easy access to information on a property of interest. With the 2012 update, every agent is now able to brand themselves—at no cost—with this app. It enables you to send your clients the app, and it strips out other agency contact info. It's truly an "individual agent branded" search experience. With its geo-local search you can "draw" a search area on your screen and it will tell you what's for sale inside the circle.

3. Redfin

The Redfin app allows you to see every home for sale, including complete home details, full-screen photos, property history and agent notes that are updated every 15 to 30 minutes. It locates nearby homes for sale, open houses and sold homes using the GPS on your iPhone or iPad.

4. Trulia

Trulia has aesthetically pleasing and functional real estate search apps. They also have an "agent app," but it's only available on iOS at the moment. It's a handy lead management tool that immediately alerts you to any incoming inquiries and allows you to manage the process inside the app.

5. Zillow

Zillow has a number of great apps across a multitude of platforms. The most powerful are its consumer facing search apps. Zillow pulls data from broker-provided feeds, MLSs, Listhub, public sources and many third-party sites. In a typical listing you'll find property data, photos, historical listing, tax data, as well as the Zillow "Zestimate."

6. ZipRealty

Their iPhone app has StreetScan technology to assist in searching, viewing and connecting in your local real estate market. StreetScan draws your search area right on the map for

a totally flexible, customized home search, and its augmented reality finds homes for sale near you. Searches can be done by zip code, location, size, recently sold, sales price, etc. It also presents home value estimates from HomeGain and eappraisal.

SUMMARY

Today's world of real estate has not only left the old way behind, it's constantly reinventing itself with new technologies and capabilities. Brokers, agents and consumers all now take for granted what not so long ago was considered the edge of technology—the Internet. Now the web is viewed as the foundational tool for launching a whole host of new applications and tools to find out everything about a property. That process—which used to take days— can now be done in seconds, and all of the related data can be instantly communicated around the world.

We've talked about and pushed for the paperless transaction for a long time and, although it has been possible for a number of years, it seems that for the first time it's actually becoming a mainstream reality and is now well within our grasp. We have agents that run the gamut from part time to full time, and we have offices that range from "traditional brick and mortar that still fully leverage paper" all the way to the other end of the spectrum, functioning as "virtual and paperless." So it appears that the only thing holding us back is the desire and commitment by everyone in the industry to make the transition.

Consumers and service providers have never had it so good. What

used to be measured in days and weeks is literally now accomplished electronically in minutes, if even that long. No longer do we have to struggle with reams of paper or the frustration of searching for a missing document. Now, everything is in the cloud. It's right there and you can access it on most electronic devices, anywhere at any time.

The next generation of client isn't likely going to settle for anything less than a fully electronic real estate transaction. Are you going to embrace or resist that shift? Are you going to ignore or leverage that opportunity? In the end it isn't a new real estate transaction we're dealing with, it's a transaction with less paper and more technology. You can do it, and you can learn to be very good at it; a knowledgeable and tech savvy paperless agent—anyplace and anytime.

Go forth, and make it happen!

About the Authors and Contributors

STEFAN SWANEPOEL

Stefan is widely recognized as the leading visionary on real estate business trends in the Unites States. He has given over 700 talks in 8 countries and 44 states to over 500,000 people and has penned 24 books and reports including:

The Amazon.com bestseller *Real Estate Confronts Reality* (1997), the highly acclaimed annual *Swanepoel TRENDS Report* (2006, 07, 08, 09, 10, 11, 12 & 13), the most recent addition to the family, the *Swanepoel TECHNOLOGY Report* (2013), and the New York Times, Wall Street Journal and USA Today bestseller *Surviving Your Serengeti: 7 Skills to Master Business & Life*.

His academic accomplishments include a bachelor's in science, a master's in business economics and diplomas in arbitration, mergers and acquisitions, real estate, computer science and marketing. His life has been a "Serengeti journey"—from his birth in Kenya to schooling in Hong Kong and South Africa to running a New York-based global franchise network with 25,000 sales associates in 30 countries. He has served as president of seven companies and two non-profit organizations.

Stefan writes, blogs and tweets throughout the year. To stay current with the latest information, where he is speaking and to reach out to him connect through one of the following sites:

Trends and Technology in Real Estate
- Website: www.retrends.com
- Twitter: www.twitter.com/retrends
- Facebook: www.facebook.com/realestatetrends

Business Fables
- Website: www.serengetibook.com
- Twitter: www.twitter.com/serengeti
- Facebook: www.facebook.com/serengeti
- YouTube: www.youtube.com/serengetibook

Speaking Engagements
- Website: www.swanepoel.com
- Twitter: www.twitter.com/swanepoel
- Facebook: www.facebook.com/swanepoel

About the Authors and Contributors

MICHAEL MCCLURE

Michael McClure is the CEO of Verified Agent, LLC, a concept that has created a CPA-like certification for the real estate industry. He is also the founder of Professional One, a real estate company based in Plymouth, MI. Michael founded RaiseTheBar Radio, a podcast focused on increasing professionalism in real estate, as well as the Raise the Bar in Real Estate Facebook Group, one of the most active online forums in real estate with nearly 3,000 of real estate's leading personalities, brokers, agents and vendors.

Michael is a nationally recognized speaker and has spoken on the topics of Twitter, Social Media, branding and professionalism at numerous conferences. Michael's Twitter (where he has approximately 55,000 followers) and other Social Media efforts have been used as training examples in the educational programs of the GoodLife Team, Keller Williams, RE/MAX, Coldwell Banker and Inman News, among others. He has developed a highly rated video training course for Twitter on Udemy.com and is a featured blogger on Inman NEXT. Michael received a degree in Accounting from Michigan State University, is a CPA and worked at Price Waterhouse for 10 years before entering real estate. He has been recognized as one of Inman News' Most Influential in Real Estate. Michael can be reached at michael@verifiedagent.com.

SEAN CARPENTER

Sean Carpenter is the Agent Development Director for the Ohio NRT companies in Columbus and Cincinnati. Originally licensed in 1998, Sean led a successful career in real estate averaging 35 transactions a year prior to assuming new duties and landing in his current role. He is the creator of the company's highly regarded PRO Start Academy and B.A.S.I.C Training sessions.

Recently named to Inman News Top 100 Most Influential Leaders in Real Estate, Sean's speaking appearances have included Coldwell Banker International Business Conferences (2007-2011), the Coldwell Banker Global Management Summit, numerous Ohio Association of REALTORS® Conventions, both the Tennessee and Virginia Association of REALTORS® Conventions and several events at various associations and Women's Council of REALTOR® events around the state of Ohio. Sean has also been the featured keynote speaker at events across the country including Chicago, St. Louis, Minneapolis, Pittsburgh, Denver, Dallas and Long Island, NY. Sean can be reached at sean.carpenter@cboki.com.

About the Authors and Contributors

JEFF LOBB

Jeff Lobb is the Vice President of Technology and Innovation at EXIT Realty Corp, Intl. He has been a Realtor® for over 23 years and has more than 10 years experience in the Internet and technology fields, both with Fortune 500® companies and start up ventures. Jeff specializes in mobile, Social Media, digital marketing and video. He has been an EXIT International Breakout speaker from 2008-2012. He is a Featured Speaker at XPLODE Real Estate Technology Conferences, and has been a speaker at RIS Media, Inman News, RETSO, Midwest Tech fair, Triple Play and WC R.

Most recently Jeff was named one of Inman News' Top 100 Most Influential Leaders in Real Estate. Jeff's expertise in real estate and technology comes from the unique experience of having been a top producing real estate professional, a brokerage owner and having a deep Internet background. Jeff can be reached at jlobb@exitrealty.com.

KELLY MITCHELL

Kelly Mitchell is a speaker, Chief Engagement Officer at PDS and the Founder/Producer of Agent Caffeine, a live weekly podcast focused on marketing, Social Media, entrepreneurship and real estate. She draws from 25+ years of strategic marketing, business development and digital marketing expertise. Her background includes successfully launching multiple startup companies, each in a unique industry, including technology and real estate. s: "Kelly has consulted for top Hawaii brands and was the inaugural President of the Social Media Club of Hawaii. She founded Next Level Hawaii, a business-centric Social Media event bringing world-class social media speakers together in Honolulu.

Kelly was responsible for acquiring a commercialization technology agreement with NASA and the development of products using NASA's DC-Tune, a digital compression algorithm. She is a sought after speaker presenting across the US and Canada on digital Marketing and Brand Management. Kelly is preparing to launch BreveTV, a weekly video cast in March 2013. Kelly can be reached at kelly@agentcaffeine.com.

CHRIS NICHOLS

Chris Nichols is the managing broker for Prudential Utah Elite Real Estate in American Fork, Utah. He has served in many capacities in the real estate industry at the national, state and local levels. In 2011 the Utah County Association of REALTORS® named Chris Realtor® of the Year, where

he also served as President. He is the 2013 Treasurer of Utah Association of REALTORS®, after serving as the dean of their Leadership Academy.

At the national level, he serves on NAR's Public Policy Coordinating Committee and as the Vice Chair of the Social Media Advisory Board. He also serves as NAR's Federal Political Coordinator to US Senator Mike Lee (UT). Chris was the very first Verified Professional Agent™ (VPA™) and has been a Social Media ambassador to several organizations at their national events. He was named one of Inman News' 100 Most Influential Real Estate Leaders for 2013. Chris can be reached at chris@utahrepro.com.

JAY THOMPSON

Jay Thompson is the Director of Industry Outreach and Social Media for Zillow, which operates the leading real estate and home-related marketplaces on mobile and the Web. Prior to joining Zillow in March of 2012 Jay was the Co-owner and Designated Broker of Thompson's Realty in Phoenix, Arizona. Jay currently splits time between Seattle and Phoenix, when he is not on the road for Zillow, speaking to real estate professionals across the country.

Jay is a frequent speaker at local, state and national real estate conferences on topics ranging from brokerage management to Social Media marketing in real estate. He built his blog, PhoenixRealEstateGuy.com, into one of the most widely-read real estate blogs in the country, and has contributed to numerous other real estate industry publications and websites.

A Summa Cum Laude Graduate of St. Edward's University in Austin, TX, Jay can be reached at jayt@zillow.com.

About the Authors and Contributors

KRISSTINA WISE

As Founder and CEO of GoodLife Team—an Austin, TX real estate firm—and Coffee with Krisstina—a national real estate training company—Krisstina Wise has spent her entire adult life working in the real estate industry. In 2008 she left the traditional real estate model behind to open her own firm and fulfill her mission to help reinvent the real estate industry and to bring it into the digital age.

Some results of her quest: in 2010 GoodLife Team was awarded "Most Innovative Brokerage" by Inman News; in 2011 GoodLife Team was featured in an Apple commercial for its innovative use of iPad for small business; in 2012 USA Today featured GoodLife Team on their Money section's front page as "a Company Gone Paperless," and, most recently, in 2013 Krisstina was named one of Inman News' 100 Most Influential Real Estate Leaders. She is also an Evernote Ambassador. Krisstina can be reached at krisstina@goodlifeteam.com.

KENDYL YOUNG

Kendyl Young is a residential Realtor® with nearly 27 years of experience and over 650 homes sold. She built her career with an obsession on marrying old fashion values with cutting edge technology. After graduating from UCLA, Kendyl worked at Proctor & Gamble for several years before leaving the corporate world in 1987 to focus on a career in real estate.

Kendyl spent most of her career as a top tier agent with Coldwell Banker before taking the title of Technology Visionary at Teles Properties in Glendale, CA in 2010. She has been featured in several industry books and articles and was named one of Inman News' 100 Most Influential Leaders in the real estate industry. She has developed a recognized expertise in technology and video, and is a respected voice in the online real estate community. She can be reached at kendyl@kendylyoung.com.

Fifteen Years of Tracking Trends
Real Estate Trends Research and Publications by Stefan Swanepoel

(2013)

(2013)

(2012)

(2011)

(2010)

(2010)

(2009)

(2008)

(2007)

(2007)

(2006)

(2006)

(2005)

(2004)

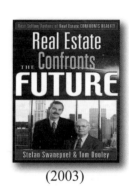
(2003)

(2003)

(2001)

(2000)

(1999)

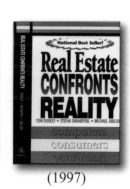
(1997)

TWO

AND THEN THERE WERE TWO

Words **80,000**

Hours of Research and Writing **1,500**

Chapters **20**

Authors **15**

Reports **2**

Source of Information **1**

The extent, speed and volume of change, innovation, shifting business models, technology and mobile advancement has resultzed in the RealSure team expanding its lineup to two annual reports.

SWANEPOEL TRENDS REPORT (164+ PAGES)

SWANEPOEL TECHNOLOGY REPORT (164+ PAGES)

April 17-19, 2013

SWANEPOEL
T3 SUMMIT
TRENDS | TECHNOLOGY | THOUGHT

- Tracking Trends
- Analyzing Impact
- Innovating Solutions
- Making A Profit

TRANSFORMING AN INDUSTRY

Stefan Swanepoel has become the custodian of American Real Estate and now also hosts the industry's premier brainstorming event.

No exhibitors. No sponsors. Only movers and shakers, leaders and rainmakers. If you like to be in the driver's seat, make a difference or be the leader of the pack - we will see you there!

" The Best Way to Predict the Future, is to Invent it. "

- Alan Curtis Kay

T3Summit.com

serengeti institute
| live | learn | survive | thrive

THE BOOK

A riveting business parable recognized as a national best seller by the New York Times, Wall Street Journal and 20 other publications and organizations. Whether you are overcoming the hardships of a brutal business environment or the struggles of life itself, you will enjoy this life fable written against the Africa safari. Published by Wiley & Sons it is available in print, audio and on the Kindle and Nook. Get your copy at www.Amazon.com

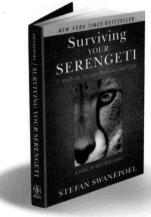

SKILLS ASSESSMENT

Over 125,000 people have taken the "What Animal Am I?" quiz. Take the first step on your journey of self-discovery with this surprisingly accurate 3-minute quiz. Discover your strongest, innate, survival skill. This free quiz can be taken at any time and as many times as you wish — online, your smartphone or via Facebook. Take the quiz at www.WhatAnimalAmI.com

TEAM BUILDING WORKSHOPS

"The Safari of Self Discovery" is a journey of introspection and personal improvement. Learning interesting behavioral and strengths about your office colleagues, team members and friends invariably leads to fun and extensive non-threatening discussions about how people work together and why we often take decisions the way we do. This fully packed, face-to-face two-day workshop is facilitated live and includes hands-on learning with many practical exercises and extensive small-group interaction. For more information visit www.SerengetiBook.com

KEYNOTE TALKS

The 90-minute keynote presentation by Stefan Swanepoel is more than a talk. It's a high-energy, stimulating experience that transports attendees into an "African Safari" with awe-inspiring visuals, stimulating stories and revealing breakthroughs. Any of the seven skills — being strategic, taking risks, being efficient, enduring, being enterprising, being good at communication and being graceful — are easily incorporated into any event and conference. To book Stefan, visit www.Swanepoel.com

LEADERSHIP SAFARIS AND RETREATS

Custom leadership retreats held according to clients' needs in both the U.S. and in the Serengeti in East Africa. Numerous retreats have already been held in the U.S. and the first retreat in the Serengeti was held February 2013.